You Are Not Alone

A Mother's Journey

To: Lana Antoine
Thank you for being so amazing to me and my Family. God bless you and your Family.
I pray this book will let you Remember how much God loves us.

Cemone Rowe

Love
Cemone
Dantae
Grace

CEMONE ROWE

You Are Not Alone
A Mother's Journey

Cemone Rowe

CEMONE ROWE

Legal Disclaimer

Copyright © 2020 Cemone Rowe

All rights reserved. No part of this publication may be reproduced or transmitted in any form or by any means, electronic, or mechanical, including photocopying, recording, or by any information storage and retrieval system.

Connect with Cemone Rowe:
Facebook: CemoneRowe
E-Mail: cemonerose@gmail.com

No part of this material may be used, reproduced, distributed or transmitted in any form and by any means whatsoever, including without limitation photocopying, recording or other electronic or mechanical methods or by any information storage and retrieval system, without the prior written permission from the author, except for brief excerpts in a review. This book is intended to provide general information only. Neither the author nor publisher provides any legal or other professional advice. If you need professional advice, you should seek advice from the appropriate licensed professional. This book does not provide complete information on the subject matter covered. This book is not intended to address specific requirements, either for an individual or an organization. This book is intended to be used only as a general guide, and not as a sole source of information on the subject matter. While the author has undertaken diligent efforts to ensure accuracy, there is no guarantee of accuracy or of no errors, omissions or typographical errors. Any slights of people or organizations are unintentional. The author and publisher shall have no liability or responsibility to any person or entity and hereby disclaim all liability, including without limitation, liability for consequential damages regarding any claim, loss or damage that may be incurred, or alleged to have been incurred, directly or indirectly, arising out of the information provided in this book.

Publisher

Connect with *Magnetic Entrepreneur Inc*

https://www.facebook.com/magneticentrepreneur

www.linkedin.com/in/magneticentrepreneur

E-Mail: info@magneticentrepreneurinc.com

Dedication

This book is dedicated to my three children. GABRIEL, who passed away after being diagnosed with anencephaly on January 18th, 2020; my firstborn son, DANTAE, who has been my rock and my biggest motivator throughout this journey; and finally, my daughter, GRACE, who inspired me to keep going even when I felt like giving up.

Anyone who has lost a child — this book is also for you, and I hope this book will help you to know that you are not alone because we are in this TOGETHER.

CEMONE ROWE

Acknowledgements

First of all, I would like to thank God because without him in my life; this book wouldn't have been possible. He was with me when no one else was, and he loved me when I couldn't even love myself. He was my strength when I was weak, and the light through my darkness, and I feel so blessed to have Him in my life. He answered my prayers when I cried for help.

Gabriel, my angel in heaven, thank you for paving the way for me because even though you are gone now, I know you are still with me today. You were the main reason why I was inspired to write this book because of the impact you made on me, your brother and sister, and so many people. Being your mom has transformed me into what God has ordained for me to be, and with your help, I am now pursuing my dream to be an author. So thank you, my son, Gabriel, in heaven. I owe this to you.

Dantae and Grace, thank you for being my biggest motivators and inspiration throughout this entire journey because even on days when I felt like giving up your guys, smiles just lit up my life. Thank you, my son, Dantae, for always encouraging me through your kind words. I remember when I told you that I was thinking about writing a book, you got so excited that where we began to write the book together, you would give me ideas for the book and motivate me by saying, "Mommy, this book is going to be amazing because you are amazing!" Even today, those words are still in my heart. You are the best son I could ever have asked for.

Facebook Mothers Group; Black Mom Connection, and more: A special thanks to everyone in these Groups who helped me to fight depression and loneliness during the darkest moments of my life. You guys reached out to me and prayed for me, in times when I wasn't able to pray for myself., You encouraged me, blessed me, and fed me. But most of all, you became a family to my children and me. You saved my life and my children's lives, which is why I have to thank God for you every day.

Gloria Neil, thank you for being the best mother to me during this very difficult time in my life. You didn't judge me or turn your back on me; instead, you stuck by my side to the end. You told me to write about my journey when you saw what I was going through, not knowing that I had already started this book. You stayed up all night with me while I wrote most nights because you believed in my dream and passion. You came to Canada not knowing what I was going through and became my rock through it all; I thank God every day that He blessed me with such an awesome mommy, and you are the best!

Maureen, you were the closest person to a family I had during my difficult pregnancy. You came into my life and stuck by my side until I laid my son to rest. I never knew a stranger could sacrifice so much for someone she'd never met, but you did. When I met you, I was battling depression and loneliness, but you came into our lives and became the sister I never had; you are indeed my chosen family.

Graciela Nicola, you have been more than a friend to me. This is why I now call you my chosen family; you have always been one of my biggest supporters in everything I do. I want to say thank you from the bottom of my heart. God sent you in my life, and you have been a blessing to my family and me. This book wouldn't even have been possible if you weren't a part of my journey. I want you to know that I cherish you from the bottom of my heart.

Dagmara, I call you my angel on earth because that is what you are to me. You also my chosen family too because, in my darkest moments from the time we met, you never left me. You made sacrifices for me in ways no one else has before, and I cherish you from the bottom of my heart. You played a huge role in writing this book, and without your help, this book wouldn't be so amazing. You inspire me, motivate me, encourage me, but above all, you believed in my talent as a bestselling author. Your two daughters are also special to me because I now see all of you as my family, including your mother too.

Facebook friends: Thanks to everyone who reached out after my son died and offered to help me raise money for his funeral. You prayed for me and also stepped in to encourage me in ways people I've known for years never did. A special thanks to Simone Simmie for the beautiful flowers and Marcia Everbless Campbell for reaching out to me and taking me out for a wonderful night. Not only did she take me out, but she made sure I was well taken care of in every way. This woman made me feel like I was her little sister, and I will never forget what she said to me that night. She said, "Cemone, after all, you been through; this is the least I could do for you because you deserve this and more."

For that one night, I wasn't dwelling on my son's death; I was feeling like a celebrity because of this lovely woman. Also, thank you, Rose Marie Sanchez for paving the way for me to meet Mr. Robert J. Moore, because without you, my book wouldn't be published right now. So thank you for bringing my dreams into reality. You are such a beautiful person inside and thank you for reaching out to me on Facebook and inviting me to be a part of Robert J. Moore's Magnetic Entrepreneur World Record Event because that day changed my life.

Mali and Ronalda: You guys took care of us in ways I never imagined was possible, you helped me through the hardest time of my life, and I thank God every day for both of you. Ronalda, you were the one who went with me to the funeral home. That touched my heart to the depth of my soul because I don't know how I could have gone through that day alone if you weren't there. You are my chosen family, that is for sure.

My midwives, **Katrina, Emily and Elizabeth** and the Mount Sinai Hospital team: You guys took care of us beyond my wildest imagination; I never knew this kind of care even existed before I met you. The love, the compassion, the comfort you showered on me made me feel like I was a celebrity under your care. My midwives helped me through depression, they comforted my heart, and they took care of me like I was family. I felt a sense of belonging with all of you, which is why choosing to go with you was the best decision I made for both my son and myself. You guys were fantastic and amazing from start to finish. Mount Sinai Hospital is the best hospital when it comes to care and compassion, hands down. Thank you all for treating me like a celebrity while I was there.

Prenatal programs and new mama friends: I was blessed to meet some wonderful mama friends through these programs who became great friends. Antoinette, thank you for introducing me to my midwives; because of you, both Gabriel and I got the best care, which was beyond imagination. Also, thanks for everything you, your mom and dad did for us, which meant a lot. Daniella, thank you for always looking out for us and for watching my children after my son died, so I could go that day with Miss Marcia

Everbless Campbell. Jamila, thank you for everything; you took care of my hair when I wasn't able to afford it. I truly appreciate it very much. You guys are special to us.

My Toronto Public health Nurse, Allie and my in-home care worker, Juliet: I thank God the day he brought you both into my life because I could never have asked for anything else from you guys. Both of you would come and listen to me when I needed to talk and never judge me or discourage me. Instead, you would motivate me and encourage me in ways beyond belief. You also helped me through depression and loneliness, but above all, you supported my dream of becoming a bestselling author. In fact, the title was approved by Juliet. Allie, you have not just been my nurse but also a friend as well. I see you guys also as my chosen family too.

My nieces Yonicia and Annalisa: Thank you for the prayers and for dropping off groceries. I truly appreciate it very much, and it means so much to us. Yonicia, you were my only family member here that looked out for me before all this happened, so I still love and respect you very much; because no matter what, you will always be special in my heart.

My Oasis family: Katie and Sarah, you have been so amazing to me in ways I do not have the words to express. I would like to thank you for the food and flowers before and after my son died, and for also coming to the hospital to sit and talk to me while I was battling depression. It truly meant a lot to me.

My Mcdonald's friends: Regina, Celine and Amara, thanks for coming to my house after my son died with a surprise I never expected in my wildest dreams. You made me so happy. Regina, a special thanks to you for believing in my dreams and helping me to make it a reality; you are amazing.

Pastor Riley and his lovely wife: Thank you for giving my son the best funeral service I could ever dream of. You were sent by God to me, along with your beautiful wife, with the voice of an angel. My son is in heaven smiling because, with your help, he got a beautiful funeral from beginning to end,

Nicole, my Photographer: Thank you for being so amazing, you have such a beautiful soul, and I thank God for you in my life. Because of you, I have so many memories of my son. You did a fantastic job at my son's funeral, and I am so grateful that you made the time to come and capture this special day for my family and me. Thank you from the bottom of my heart.

Beverly Howe thank you for supporting my dreams and always checking in on me, that truly means so much to my family and me.

CEMONE ROWE

Pat, thank you for being such an amazing editor; you are so patient and understanding; you are one of a kind. It's been a pleasure to work with you.

Robert J Moore: Thank you for believing in me as a bestselling author and choosing to help me make this dream become a reality; you are amazing. I am so honoured to have met you in person at your Magnetic Entrepreneur Guinness World Record event because I knew that day you would become my publisher one day.

Table of Contents

Table of Contents

DEDICATION
.........v

ACKNOWLEDGEMENTS...vii
Table of Contents xv
FOREWORD..xvii
Introduction..xix
Chapter 1..1
THE NEWS THAT CHANGED MY LIFE FOREVER...............1
Chapter 2..11
FACEBOOK MOTHERS' GROUP......................................11
Chapter 3..27
RECEIVING THE BEST CARE DURING MY PREGNANCY....27
Chapter 4 39
THE ARRIVAL OF MY MOTHER IN CANADA 39
Chapter 5..51
LIFE AND DEATH DECISION..51
Chapter 6..59
THE DEATH OF MY SON GABRIEL................................59
Chapter 7..65
DELIVERING MY STILLBORN SON 65
Chapter 8..77
FUNERAL ARRANGEMENTS 77

Cemone Rowe
Chapter 9..*97*

Foreword

It is both an honour, and a privilege to write the foreword for *You Are Not Alone*. Having been personally affected by the deaths of so many of my loved ones, I can identify with the thoughts and emotions Cemone expresses so powerfully in this book.

This is much more than a self-help book dealing with health adversity. Cemone Rowe, a woman of faith, details her journey through her baby, Gabriel's diagnosis of Anencephaly and demonstrates that God is able to work in our lives during the worst of situations and answer prayer.

Even though Cemone was abandoned by her family and friends as she went through a very difficult pregnancy and faced exhaustion and depression, she never gave up on wanting to give Gabriel life, although from the outset, the prognosis was that he would not survive.

Cemone's love, care and dedication to her other two children, Dantae and Grace, never wavered even though she had no support until God brought just the people she needed into her life.

Cemone's dependence on God has affected a huge number of people, and will continue to grow as her circle of

CEMONE ROWE

influence grows because of her desire to help others by her story.

If you have lost a child, this book will help you see that you are not alone.

Robert J. Moore

5X International Best-Selling Author

Founder and CEO of Magnetic Entrepreneur Inc.™

Guinness World Record Holder

INTRODUCTION

As you have chosen to read my book, I know it will change your life and touch your heart in ways you can never imagine are even possible because that is how powerful and incredible my journey was, and still is even today, after my son Gabriel is gone.

This book will teach you about love, patience, obedience, faith, trusting God, and how powerful it is to pray, family, selflessness, long-suffering, loneliness, and so much more. Above all, it will help you to understand that even though you may feel like you are alone in this world, just remember, you are never truly alone because someone out there is waiting to help you. All you need to do is seek it.

You Are Not Alone is a book that I got inspired to write to the world about my incredible journey as an anencephaly mom because of the hardship I encountered while carrying my son Gabriel.

He melted the hearts of thousands of people on social media without even entering this world alive, and that is when I realized how powerful his story was, which is why I decided to write this book.

All my life, I have struggled with loneliness, but it wasn't until this pregnancy journey with my son Gabriel.

that I encountered firsthand what loneliness was — and what it felt like to be completely alone in the world.

I was going through one of the darkest times of my life, and before I gained the courage to seek help, I felt as if I had no one to turn to at all, and that drove me deep into depression.

I needed help, but I didn't know where to look because I was so afraid of being judged, criticized or putting my children in danger, that I decided to face the world alone.

Many people told me throughout my lifetime that I was a very strong woman, but I never saw it until I was left to fight depression while pregnant and raising my other two children completely alone with no support from family or friends. They thought they were there for me, but without being there physically to help me, I was suffering and struggling so much, and that drove me deeper into depression.

This book will inspire you to be strong despite what you are going through in your life because even though I was pregnant, depressed and raising two children all alone, I never gave up on any of my children; instead, I was willing to give up my own life just to give my son Gabriel life.

My aim is to use this book not only to inspire people never to give up on their loved ones, but also to teach people how important it is to follow their hearts and stand up for what is best for them. In the end, the decisions we make will determine the outcome of how we will get through the worst possible situations.

I have encountered many unthinkable experiences throughout my life, both growing up in Jamaica and here in Canada, which have left scars both emotionally and physically. Despite all that I have gone through, nothing could compare to the death of my son. His death didn't just change my life, but it also transformed me inside and out in ways I never thought were even possible.

My journey with him has helped me to overcome fear and given me the fortitude to go for everything I was afraid to do all my life.

I know you must be wondering, what has Cemone been through before? Well, here are a few things: at age 14, I was raped by a close family friend in Jamaica, and I carried this burden with me for almost 17 years before actually sharing it without crying because even today, it still hurts me to think about what took place that day.

At age 17, I was molested by someone close to the family. Even though my family knew about it, no one tried to help me through it, so I ran away and went to a shelter where I completed high school.

During that time, I experienced firsthand what it felt like to be hungry because, at times, I would go to bed without food, then I would go to school the next day with my belly making noise in class because I needed food and couldn't afford it.

I have been through more than one abusive relationship, where at one point, I had to run away to Jamaica to fight my depression.

I had been through more than an average person by the age of 32, but nothing moved me the way the death of my son did. His journey pushed me to my limits, took so much out of me emotionally, physically, mentally, and spiritually, but above all, it tested my trust and faith in God in ways I never thought were even possible.

My experiences with my son have opened up my eyes in so many ways because I was blind to a lot of things. Now I have learned to cherish every moment as if it's my last because life is too short to take anything or anyone for granted.

My son, Gabriel's journey, made me realize how powerful social media is, and it allowed me to create my own family that I always wanted all my life.

When I had no one around me, I had a family on Facebook that supported me more than the people I knew all my life through my darkest moments here on earth.

They laughed with me and cried with me; they stood by me from the day I shared the news of my son to the day I laid him to rest. Even today, I am getting support from them.

Some of the greatest people in my life today are people I met through my journey with Gabriel. I decided to call them my chosen family because they were all chosen by God to come into my life, not when I wanted them, but when God knew I needed them to be there.

This book will let you know how important it is to pray and trust God, but most importantly, the necessity of being obedient to the voice of God when he speaks to us.

I always wonder what would have happened if I had chosen to disobey God, but I will save that for another book in the future.

This book was written for everyone, even if you do not believe in God. So if you do not believe in God, that is perfectly fine because I am not here to convince anyone or force religion on anyone who is reading my book, but instead, I want to help people find the light at the end of the tunnel.

By reading this book, I hope it will encourage someone who is going through a very dark moment to know that they are not alone because there is always help available for everyone in this world. At times we have to go and seek it and just hope and pray for the right help to find us.

I have no doubt in my mind that this journey was designed to happen because God knows my heart, and he knew I would not fail the test, which is why I was rewarded with so much blessing beyond my imagination.

This book will make you cry, but not only that, it will also touch your heart beyond words as you use your imagination to comprehend how powerful you can be if only you chose to do what is best for you and the ones you love the most.

Walking away from my OB was one of the best decisions I ever made during my pregnancy because it was through that decision I was able to receive the best care during my pregnancy, which was above and beyond my prayers and expectations.

God turned impossibilities into possibilities when he intervened on my behalf and made it possible for my mom to come to Canada, not when I wanted her, but when I needed her because God's timing is the best.

You will witness what it means to have unconditional love for someone and how selfless one mother can be in this world. I know many people will relate to this book because the love of a mother cannot be compared to anything, and this book proves it to the world.

The death of a child is one of the hardest things anyone could ever go through in this life, especially if you are the mother. After everything we endure physically, mentally, and emotionally, if our baby is taken from us, that alone could make someone want to end their own life.

Imagine going through almost nine months of pain and suffering, then one day, to be told, "I am sorry, but there is no heartbeat." This was my story. At that moment, I wanted to die too, but I knew I had my other two children to live for, so I had to fight really hard to stay strong, not for me, but for them.

Just imagine going through 48 hours of induced labour only to deliver a baby who has no life. At that moment, my heart was so broken to the point where I couldn't even find tears to cry. Instead, I started to pray for strength to keep going, because deep down, I felt like my heart was going to stop. Not many people will understand how difficult it was to hold my son in my arms for the first time, knowing that he will not cry or open his eyes because he was gone.

Imagine walking into a hospital pregnant and walking out with no baby. That day, as I was leaving, I felt as if my heart was going to drop out of my chest onto the floor, but I thank God for all the people he sent into my life because they are the main reason why I got through those dark moments.

Sometimes, I will not lie; I questioned God and even gave up on believing in Him at one point because I couldn't understand how He could love me but allow all these things to happen to me over and over again.

I remember, I even stopped going to church, stopped praying, stopped believing, but what I failed to realize was that even when I stopped loving Him, He never stopped loving me. Many times, I should have died, but He always saved my life, because he had a purpose for me. Now, as I am writing this book, and the impact I have made over the years, makes me realize what God's purpose is for me in this world.

I am here to use my life's stories and experiences to impact others by inspiring people who need it, motivate those who are about to give up, heal those who are hurt and broken and encourage you never to give up no matter what life brings your way.

Reading this book will unleash the real you because you not weak; instead, you are stronger than you think. You are not alone; in fact, you are loved beyond words; you do not have to do things because someone tells you it's best for you. Rather, choose to do whatever you can live with because, in the end, your final decision will affect you the most, and the last thing you want is to live with regrets.

Sometimes, life will force you to make some heartbreaking decisions that will have you crying for days but do not rush it. Allow yourself to feel everything and then with a clear mind, make a final decision that you know is right for you, one that can help you to heal, one that brings you peace but most of all, one that you will be able to live with for the rest of your life.

At my son's funeral, while carrying him for the last time, I was smiling, and no one could understand why. In their minds, they were all wondering how a person could still find the strength to smile after everything she went through. My smile didn't come because I wasn't feeling hurt, nor did it come because the journey was easy; instead, I smiled because I knew in my heart, I had done everything humanly possible for my son, even after his own father walked away from us. I smiled because I knew I had done my part, and now he was with his Heavenly Father. I had no regrets, so the peace of God was with me, and therefore I was able to smile through the storm.

The hardest part for me through this entire journey wasn't the pain and suffering, but instead, it was sitting in his funeral service, watching him in that little box, then carrying him in my arms for the very last time to his final resting place and watching him go down in that grave, knowing that I would never see him again. That was what made me want to die with him right there. I wanted to go down in the grave with him, but I had my other two children to live for, so I had to say goodbye to him.

CEMONE ROWE

I would like to leave this poem with you, and I hope that as you read it, it will heal your pain and uplift your spirit, knowing that you are not alone because someone always cares, even if, at times, you may not see or feel it.

You are not alone

I may not be able to take away your pain

But I am here to tell you that someone does care

When you feel like your whole world is falling apart

Always remember that God is holding you in his arms

When you want to talk but no one is near

Just remember that God is just a prayer away

Don't be afraid to cry when you are hurting

Because that is a sign to God that you need him there

Hold on to your faith even on your hardest days

Because in the midst of the storm, God will put a smile on your face

So do not worry and never be afraid

Because in the midst of your darkness, God will be your light

Chapter 1

The News that Changed my Life Forever

I remember this day like it was just yesterday because it was a beautiful sunny Friday afternoon. I was at home trying to get everything done before I had to get my two children from school and daycare. I had spent that day running errands and doing chores because the weekend was fast approaching. I knew that when I had my kids with me on weekends, it was impossible to get anything done, especially with my little daughter Grace, since she is a handful, or let's just say she is very attached to mommy. My daughter gives me headaches at times, but she is so precious, which is why I always spoil her with lots of hugs and kisses. I can't resist being affectionate around them; I love my children to the moon and back with all of my heart and soul.

My son Dantae, on the other hand, is my little helper, he is very caring and compassionate towards me, and he always knows how to put a smile on my face, even on my worst days. He is by far the best son I could ever have asked for. Everyone who knows him is drawn to him because he has the personality of a real gentleman., Not only that, but he takes such good care of his sister at home and wherever else we go as a family. This alone makes me feel so blessed to be their mother.

Being a single mother to them has been super challenging for me because, over the past few years, I have had little or no support from anyone raising them. That includes family and friends. I remember, at times, it got so overwhelming and exhausting doing everything alone that I just had to sit down and cry to myself while I prayed to God for strength to keep on going.

That Friday afternoon, I had just finished cooking dinner and decided to have some me-time before the kids got home when I heard my phone ringing; the caller ID read that it was my doctor. I answered the phone, and I was told, "Your results are in, and you need to come ASAP to see the doctor because he needs to speak with you, urgently." After I got off the phone, my heart started to race, and that's when I knew something was definitely wrong. Anyway, I got dressed, and I took the bus there. Upon arrival, I stood outside the door and prayed for strength to face the news, which was about to change my life forever.

I went in, and the look on the lady's face when she saw me made my heart skip a beat because deep down, I knew something was really wrong with my baby. She had known me for many years because I started going there while I was pregnant with my son Dantae who is turning nine this year.

I sat there for over two hours before I got to see my doctor, and immediately when he walked in the room, just the look upon his face again made my heart skip another beat. I tried to convince myself it wasn't going to be as bad as I thought, but unfortunately, it was even worse than I could ever have imagined.

That day I was told my baby was showing signs of what they called Anencephaly because, based on his ultrasound, they could not see a brain or a skull developing fully. I sat there in shock, not knowing how to even respond because before this news, I didn't even know this was even possible during pregnancy. I had never heard of this diagnosis before, which is one of the reasons why I insisted on them doing another one to confirm this heartbreaking news.

Furthermore, even though I didn't want to believe this terrible news about my baby, and in my heart, I wished they were all wrong, I just couldn't help myself from breaking down into tears right in front of both of them. At that moment, I was so overwhelmed with emotion because not only did I have a baby that may not be born alive (approximately 75% of babies with Anencephaly are stillborn), but I was already struggling as a single mother with my other two children.

To add to this stress, when I found out I was pregnant and had shared the news with a few close family and friends, including his father, they didn't seem to care. Based on their response, I then regretted even telling them at all. So with everything going on already, I was just not prepared emotionally or mentally for anything else that would add more stress to my life.

I sat there for over ten minutes, with tears running down my cheeks as I tried to convince myself that this was all a mistake. Perhaps at my next ultrasound, my baby would be healthy. They left me in the room while I cried, and moments later, I dried my tears and walked out of the office, hoping in my heart that this was just a misunderstanding. But unfortunately, it was indeed reality, based on a few more ultrasounds.

After I left the office, I went outside, and I sat down for almost an hour crying again because my heart could not accept the news I had just received about my baby. I cried so much that afternoon that my eyes were red, and my head hurt like crazy. Even though I was struggling with my other two kids, a part of me was still very happy knowing I was going to have another beautiful baby. The mind sometimes will deny the facts and believe what it wants. My son, Dantae, had always wanted a little brother, so in my heart, I thought this was a perfect gift to surprise him with once I knew the gender.

My heart was so broken that afternoon to the point where I wanted to tell someone about the hurt and pain I was feeling, but I had no one to even confide in since everyone I knew was already against my pregnancy. I felt so alone and confused, not knowing how to even face the rest of that day. But because of my children, I had to find the strength I needed to fight my emotions and pretend I was okay in order to be able to take care of them without falling apart.

Later that evening, after I went to pick up my children from daycare and we got home, I really wished I had some kind of help or support at home waiting for me because for the first time, in a very long time, I just wanted to go to bed and wished this day was only a dream. Since that wasn't the case, I had to put all my hurt and feelings aside and focus on caring for my two children.

The next day when I got up, I decided to share my heartbreaking news with the father of my baby, even though I knew from our last conversation that he wasn't happy about the baby. What happened after I told him took me by surprise. He told me never to call or text his phone again. He continued by saying these exact words, "I don't want no sick baby; I already have enough stress in my life." At first, I was angry and frustrated because I didn't want to face this alone, but unfortunately, that is exactly what happened. In the end, until God intervened on my behalf.

I also shared the news with a few other people, which included family, friends and even the church I was going to, but no one reached out to help or support me. As time went by, I got depressed by having to face everything alone while taking care of my kids, to the point where I couldn't eat or sleep properly. As a result, I was always feeling sick and very weak.

This is when I realized that I really needed help desperately. But I didn't know where to get the help I needed, since everyone I thought would have been there for me decided to turn away. My next ultrasound was scheduled in three weeks to confirm whether or not the baby had Anencephaly. The thought of going there alone brought tears to my eyes.

Every night before I went to bed, I would cry to God for help. I needed emotional support to get through this, and I had no idea where to get it. Suddenly, I remembered the mothers' group I had joined on Facebook, and that is when it hit me. Maybe I could share my story there and see if anyone could relate to what I am going through. Maybe, just maybe, someone would reach out to me and help me get through this horrible nightmare.

I won't lie; at first, I was very skeptical about sharing my personal life on social media for many reasons. I knew, based on my own life experiences in the past, how judgmental and heartless some people can be regardless of what you are going through. Not only that, but I was very concerned about how it could affect my two children if something bad were to happen along the way.

Nevertheless, I decided to swallow my pride and ignore my fear as I wrote my story on my phone. Before I shared my story in the mothers' group, I found myself praying to God for guidance and protection because my greatest desire was to be connected only to good-hearted people, who were sent by God to help me through this difficult journey of my life.

After I posted my story in the mothers' group, and it got approved, I was completely blown away by all the comments that were coming in on my phone. Immediately, I got very emotional to the point where I just started to cry. Even though I had made no connection in the first couple of days, I was just so overjoyed because without even knowing me, people were so concerned about my two children and me along with my unborn child. That alone touched my heart very deeply.

I remember just sitting there reading each comment, and to be honest; it helped me so much emotionally to overcome my depression. I began to focus on the fact that I am not completely alone. I would stay up at night when I was unable to sleep and just read all the comments. Without a doubt in my mind, I knew something amazing was going to happen someway and somehow because I felt it deep in my heart.

Every day in the morning, when I got up, I was praying that God would intervene by connecting me to someone.

For a couple of days, nothing had happened, but that never affected my faith and trust in God. I trusted strongly that he would come through for me at the right time. That is what kept me going regardless of how I felt otherwise.

There were days when I felt so emotionally exhausted and physically drained because I wasn't eating well. Neither was I sleeping well, and I was caring for my two children all alone.

The strength it took to get through my depression wasn't easy, but I fought hard every day to get through it because I knew I had my children to love and care for, regardless of how I felt. Because of my faith and trust, God came through for me, not when I wanted him to, but when he knew I needed him most.

Something amazing happened one week before my second ultrasound appointment. I was going through the mothers' group comments, and suddenly, I received a message through Facebook messenger. To my surprise, a mother from the group reached out to me and what she wrote in her message brought me to tears because I knew God had answered my prayers.

Many times in our lives, we feel like giving up or giving in because we are not supported in the way we hoped and wished. But I am here to tell you that once you believe and trust in the will of God, he will always make a way for you.

I am aware that not everyone reading my book believes in God, which is very understandable, but in order to make it through something tragic, we must find something to believe in that is far beyond our greatest imagination. Knowing that whatever we choose to believe in will not let us down when we are in need of help the most, is a great comfort. My strength and will to carry on after everything that had happened wasn't from me, but instead, it was from my Father up above.

Lastly, please seek help when you need it despite what others may say about reaching out to strangers, because many times in my life, not just in this pregnancy, but in other areas of my life, God has used strangers to help me rather than my own family. Don't get me wrong; we must always be careful from whom we choose to accept help. This is why I find time to pray to God first, before I choose to seek help from anyone. Furthermore, if you don't believe in prayer, you could find something else in which you trust to lead the way for you and hope that it will guide and protect you, as I did.

Here is a very powerful quote that I came up with, which I would like to leave with you today. I hope just as it added meaning to my life over the years, it will do the same for you too. And it reads,

CEMONE ROWE

"Don't be afraid to seek help when you need it, instead be more afraid to suffer in silence because that will surely destroy you in the end." - Cemone Rowe.

Chapter 2

Facebook Mothers' Group

Her name was Maureen, the lovely mama who reached out to me that day. In her message, she said, "I read your story, and it touched my heart so deeply, and I knew I had to reach out to you because no one should have to go through what you're going through alone." She then continued by saying, "I am not in Canada right now, but I will be back in the next two days, so if it's okay with you, I would like to come with you to your next ultrasound appointment. Please let me know when it is, and I will be there."

I replied to her thanking her for reaching out to me, and I gave her the date of my ultrasound, as she requested. For some reason, in my heart, I knew she was sent to me by God because I felt a calm spirit within me as I wrote each message to her that day. The very next day, I received another message from another mother in the group. She was a doula (one who helps in birth), and after reading my story, she also wanted to connect with me and offered her service to me free of charge. Not only that, but she also offered to come with me to my ultrasound appointment as well.

The name of this group is called BMC, which stands for Black Mom Connection and to be honest, it has been a blessing in my life in ways I never imagined were even possible. Not only did I meet a few wonderful mamas there, but this group also became someplace safe for me to share my difficult pregnancy journey. Everyone in the group was so loving, caring, and compassionate towards what I was going through, and not only that, they were all praying for me and uplifting my spirit in ways I wouldn't have been able to do on my own.

Two days before my ultrasound appointment, I received another message from the doula asking for the location of the appointment, so I replied with the details and thanked her once again for being so nice to me. I also received a message from Maureen the night before my appointment, asking for my address because she wanted to bring me to the appointment. That night, for the first time, I actually slept a little bit better, knowing that God had sent me some support, which meant I wouldn't have to face that day alone. That morning I got up, and I started to pray to God in my heart, hoping to receive good news at my ultrasound appointment while I was getting the kids ready for daycare.

Around 8:45 a.m., I received a message from Maureen, telling me she was in front of my house. Because she was extra early, I told her we were still getting ready and then she replied by saying to me, "That's okay, take your time, no rush. I will still be here waiting for you." She then drove me to drop my kids off at their daycare, and then we headed to my appointment. On the way, I received a text from the doula saying she was on her way there, and I replied to her, "See you soon."

While we were talking on the way there, in my heart, I felt like I knew her for years because there was such peace and realness between us. We were talking and laughing like she had been my friend for years, and that's when it hit me. I am not alone anymore, and I knew right there and then that no matter what happened that day, I would have support from that day forward.

We arrived at my appointment, and immediately as I approached the door to go in, my heart felt heavy, not knowing what the result was going to be. But I knew one thing for sure, that no matter what had happened that day, I will love my baby, and nothing will ever change that. They called me in for the ultrasound, and while he was doing it, based on his facial expression, I knew something was definitely wrong, but, in my heart, I was hoping I was just overthinking it, so I decided just to trust God instead.

After my ultrasound, I met the doula. We greeted each other, and we all left the office. At that moment, I wanted to cry, but I held back my tears because I am not one to show my emotion in front of people. We went back to Maureen's car, and they suggested we get something to eat. While we were eating, I got a call from my OB office saying I had an appointment that same day, so I mentioned it to them, and they offered to go there too with me.

My ultrasound appointment had been changed at the last minute, which is why they ended up on the very same day. But I didn't remember about my OB appointment until I got the call from the office. We later arrived for my OB appointment, and after waiting for almost one hour, Maureen decided to ask the person at the front desk if it was possible to request my ultrasound result from the ultrasound office, and she agreed to try and get it for us.

After like an hour, she then confirmed that they had received it, and my OB would give me the result when I went in to see him. I sat there so worried, but also very thankful I wasn't there alone. Unfortunately, based on time, the doula had to leave because she had another appointment, so I thanked her for coming, and she left.

A few minutes later, I was called in, and I decided to bring Maureen in with me as my support person because I knew I wasn't in the right mindset to answer any questions. She would be doing that for me, and I must admit she was better than I could have ever expected her to be from start to finish.

I remember, when my OB walked in, he was surprised to see me with someone there because in the eight years he had known me, he had never seen me with a support person before, except for my son while I was pregnant with my daughter. I remember he then asked me who she was, and she replied, "I am her sister, her friend and everything that she needs right now." I must admit those words touched my heart so deeply; I almost started to cry, then we looked at each other and smiled.

After he checked my results, he confirmed that indeed my son Gabriel was diagnosed with Anencephaly. Based on the information he received, unfortunately, he was diagnosed with the worst kind in history, which meant he would not survive after he was born.

She then asked him a few questions, and he concluded by saying, "In his opinion, termination would be the best option for me, because according to how severe his diagnosis is, he believes it would be less painful for me in the end, based on his past experience with other people." He never asked me how I felt; neither did he show any compassion or sensitivity toward me, knowing that I was about to lose my baby according to his results.

He then asked me to collect the abortion paper at the front desk, and then he said, "Good luck," Upon leaving his office, he told the person at the front desk to give me the abortion papers so that I could call them back and make an appointment to terminate the baby. She then handed me the papers, and I knew I didn't have the heart to take his life, but on top of that, I wasn't going to go back to my OB's office ever again.

At that very moment, I knew that I was not going to end his life as my OB suggested, but instead, I was going to love him and cherish him for as long as I could no matter what, because I knew deep down in my heart he was worthy of being loved even if it was just by me. After that day, I never went back there because not only was I disappointed with how he treated me that day, I also knew that he would have never provided me with the kind of care I needed going forward with my pregnancy.

Maureen and I walked back to her car, where I sat to process the news I had just received. Even though I felt so heartbroken by this terrible news, I also felt so blessed knowing that I didn't have to face it alone, thanks to a wonderful stranger who was now my friend.

She was so loving and compassionate towards me, and that made me realize how amazing God was in the time I really needed his help the most. She then drove me back to my kid's daycare, allowing me to pick them up, dropped us off, and then gave me a big hug upon leaving. I will never forget what she said to me that evening; she told me that if I ever needed anything, I should not be afraid to reach out to her and that she would try her best to be there for both my children and me in any way she could. Believe it or not, but right there and then, I knew I was not alone.

The next day I received another message from another mama in the same group inviting me to church. Her message was so filled with hope, faith, and compassion towards me, so I decided to accept her invitation. In her message, she said, "I know it will be difficult for you to come to my church with your two children, so if it's okay with you, I will come and pick you and the kids up and also drop you off after church." She kept her word, and for the first time in a long time, I wasn't afraid to face anything. In fact, in my heart, I knew that regardless of what happened with my baby, in the end, God will be glorified.

A couple of days later, I decided to share my story again in a few other mothers' groups because I wanted to see if anyone could relate to my son's diagnosis with Anencephaly. But unfortunately, unlike the first group, these ones had some heartless and judgmental mothers. As a mother, I thought they would have been compassionate and less judgmental, but unfortunately, I was so wrong. In fact, they were so heartless and mean to me, to the point where it started to affect me emotionally again. I had to pray so hard and trust God to get me through it.

I desperately wanted to leave that group because my spirit was so disturbed, but something in my spirit kept on saying, "Do not leave," and I obeyed that little voice. To my surprise, guess what happened next? God let me meet two more wonderful mama friends in that same group.

CEMONE ROWE

I remember receiving a message from this lovely mama named Grace, and immediately it was like our spirits were connected to each other. Her name stood out to me because she had the same name as my daughter, and based on our conversation deep down; I knew she was also sent by God. She invited me out for coffee a few days later, and just like Maureen, when I met her, both of us felt like we had known each other for years; it was so natural and real.

I remember that day very well because she came to pick me up from a prenatal program that Thursday. I could never forget that morning because I gave her the wrong address since it was my first time attending that program. She took a while to find me, but when she drove up to me, and I got in her car, we hugged and then we just started laughing because we were both so happy to finally meet in person.

She took me for coffee, and we sat there and talked for almost two hours, just getting to know each other and to be honest, I knew within my heart just by talking with her that she was also sent by God to help me through the darkest days of my pregnancy. The very next day, I got a message from her saying she felt led by God to reach out to me after she read my story. She went on to say that she has never reached out to anyone before, but she just had to take a chance with me.

We continued talking almost every day since we have met, and she offered to get me groceries the second time we met. She has also volunteered her time to come to my apartment and help me clean up, after she saw that I was unable to do anything based on the size of my belly. She has done more for me in less than a month than people I knew all of my life. To be honest, that really changed my way of thinking when it comes to meeting a stranger.

We were told many times during our lives never to accept help from strangers because they are evil. But what they forget to mention is that not everyone is the same because in everything there will be good and bad. When we pray and ask for protection, God will only bring the right people our way, and yes, I am speaking from experience because this is my own personal life story you are reading right now.

Every day I received lots of comments on my story; most of them were good, but a few were very negative. I also received a few messages from people in different groups; some were motivational, others were encouraging, a few were negative, but most of them were uplifting. That alone was enough for me, just knowing that people cared about me so much without even knowing me in person, gave me so much hope to keep on going, no matter what the devil tried to bring my way.

A few weeks later, I got so sick at home while taking care of my two children, and because one of my greatest weaknesses was not asking for help. But for some strange reason, that day, something led me to share it in the same group that I had met Grace a couple of weeks before, so I obeyed my gut feeling, and I decided to share what I was going through. Moments later, I saw many people praying for me in the comments below my post, asking God to give me the strength I needed to keep going, no matter what, and to keep on being the strong and amazing mother that I am to my children.

A few minutes later, this lovely mama reached out to me. Her name was Dagmara, and to my surprise she offered to come babysit my kids so I could rest. Even though in the eight years of being a mother I have never trusted any one, including family, to take my kids without me going with them, something about her felt different in my heart. I told her yes without even thinking twice at that moment.

She lived very far from me, so after I accepted her offer, she then told me to get them ready, and she would be there in two hours or less. After like an hour, the devil started to play with my mind telling me a lot of foolishness, but then I prayed and asked God to take over my mind and also my life.

Thirty minutes later, she told me she was ten minutes away, and right then and there, I almost chickened out because I am so protective of my children to the point where I don't even allow them to go with their own father anywhere without me. Being with him for nine years helped me to develop trust issues towards him because not only was he careless and irresponsible, he just didn't take anything seriously, which is why we broke up. He doesn't pay child support to help me raise them, neither does he try to change his ways in order to gain my trust and try to build a relationship with his children.

Anyway, she arrived at my place and knocked on my door. As soon as I saw her and her two daughters, I knew everything was going to be okay. She then told me she was going to take them to the Mc Donald's only just five minutes from my house so that I could get at least one to two hours to myself to rest. I didn't even care how I looked because I was so tired and exhausted; all I needed was a little rest. During the time that she had them, she kept sending me pictures and videos until I dozed off. Then, one hour later, I woke up and checked my phone, and all I could do was smile because they were having a blast without me, and for the first time in a very long time, I wasn't afraid of seeking help. Instead, I was more afraid of suffering in silence, all alone.

Don't get me wrong, with everything I do in life, I always pray first, and I always listen to my inner spirit. She wasn't the only one who offered to help me with my kids, but as I mentioned before, if my spirit doesn't lead me to accept your help, it doesn't matter how I feel, or how desperately I may need help, my heart would accept the help because nothing is more important to me in this life than my children.

She brought them back almost two hours later, and she gave me a hug. I could tell she was very nervous by the look in her eyes, but regardless of how she felt, she still came to help me out when I needed it the most. That opened my eyes to see something amazing, which is that there are many good people in this world who are willing to help if only we find the courage to ask at times instead of choosing to suffer alone in silence.

I texted her later on that evening, and I thanked her for everything. I even told her that she was an angel sent by God, and that is when she confessed to me that after she saw my post, something led her to reach out to me. She continued by saying at first, she was so scared because she had never done this before, and she was afraid of getting in danger. She continued by saying that after she told her daughters, they panicked and said to her, "Mommy, are you crazy? You don't know her, why would you want to just go and help a stranger like that? It is not safe." and on top of that, after she told her friends what she was about to do, they were all against it, but she said something in her heart kept on saying, "Go help her, she really needs your help." And as hard as it was, she decided to obey the voice speaking to her, and that is how she ended up at my house that day.

If I may add, her daughters blew me away when I saw how caring and compassionate they were with my children. It just melted my heart; they took such good care of my almost-three-year-old daughter to the point where people would have thought they were related. They also played with my son as if we were one big happy family. That made me realize how powerful God can be when we choose to trust him and allow Him to be in control of our lives. Her two daughters' names are Selina and Sara; they are just a few years older than my son, which is why they bonded together so well.

I also confessed to her about how the devil was playing with my mind telling me things like she was going to steal my kids and that I am a bad mother for allowing my kids to go with a stranger I met online. And that he even made me feel guilty for sharing my story and accepting help, but in my heart, there was a voice saying to me, "You have asked for help, and now I am sending the help you need, so please trust me."

After that day, I had no doubt in my mind that God was with me, and even though it has been a very difficult journey, at least I wasn't alone anymore because I had some mamas by my side to help me through some of my darkest days.

Let me leave this with you. Trusting anyone in this life can be very scary, and yes, it is a risk, but not only that, it will make you feel guilty at first, which is natural because we are indeed human beings and especially if you are a mother, that makes it even worse. But keep in mind that it takes a village to raise a child, which means you do not have to face that journey alone.

There are many resources available out there, which I only learned about during this journey of my life because I chose to share my story with the world instead of keeping it to myself. I have never been the kind of person who feels comfortable approaching people and asking for help, which is why I felt more safe sharing it in the mothers' groups because I knew at least one person would have reached out to me at some point in time. Most of all, I trusted God that he would only send the right people my way.

Only you know what's best for you and what approach is more comfortable for you, so, therefore, you can seek help how it suits you, but remember, in everything, there is good and bad so just make sure you are careful when reaching out for help. As we all know, this world is very scary and judgmental at times, but regardless of that, do not suffer alone. Reach out for help someway or somehow because depression is a killer, and I wouldn't want anyone to be a victim of it when there is so much help available in this world.

Just follow your gut feeling and trust your heart that when you seek help, the right help will come to you and remember, you don't have to do it alone.

CEMONE ROWE

Chapter 3
Receiving the Best Care During my Pregnancy

Since I was attending a few prenatal programs while I was pregnant on days where I wasn't feeling weak or too sick to go out, I was referred to a Toronto Public Health Nurse whose name was Allie. At first, to be honest, it took me a while to even connect with her because I didn't feel comfortable talking about my baby's condition with anyone face to face. It was just too painful for me having someone looking at me while I express my emotions, which is why I was more comfortable sharing my story in the mothers' group vs in real life.

Anyway, as time went by, my spirit led me to call her and book the appointment. I won't lie; I was so nervous and scared about meeting her that every day I would pray so hard, hoping she would be nice when I met her. I remember the first time she showed up at my door. I looked through the glass of my door, and I said to myself, "Should I open it or not?" I got so nervous because I knew I would have to tell her about my baby's condition, and I wasn't ready for that, but something said, "Cemone, just open the door, it will all be okay," so I listened and opened it, and invited her in.

While we were there talking, I realized how sweet, caring, and compassionate she was and immediately, I felt bad for waiting so long to connect with her in the first place. But nevertheless, as we continued to talk more, I realized we shared a lot in common, including being a single mother and raising children while pregnant. I was so amazed by her story and the strength she had within her to overcome that, and I guess that's why I liked being around her as much as I did.

She was so inspiring and encouraging to me, especially after I told her about my life and my baby's condition; the way she enlightened me every time we met gave me so much motivation not to give in or give up on my son, and that's when I realized I was so blessed to have her in my life.

Allie got so concerned about me that she offered to find a home care worker for me, so I had someone here to talk to at times when I am unable to go to prenatal programs because I am very weak at times, more often than I should be. Her name was Juliet. She was also a blessing in my life too because just like Allie, she never made me feel guilty about my decision to carry my son due to his diagnosis; instead she always encouraged me to make a decision I am able to live with and that I should always follow my heart because, in the end, the decision I make will only affect my children and me the most and no one else because I am his mother and they are his siblings, which means we love him the most in this world and indeed she was right 100%.

The next week I went to a prenatal group, and I met a few pregnant women. Two of them, for some reason, my spirit just connected with, and we started talking. The following week my spirit led me to tell one of them about my baby's condition. At first, I was very nervous, but that voice kept saying talk to her she can help you. Anyway, I told her about what I was going through that Thursday, and the following week she invited me to her house since she lives only five minutes away from where the program we went to that day was held.

Furthermore, upon arriving at her house, I met her lovely mother, and she told me her name was Gabriella. Then I replied to her and said, my name is Cemone, and she then asked me, "Are you having a boy or a girl?" I replied to her that "It's a boy based on his ultrasound," so immediately she smiled and said to me, "You should name him Gabriel." Then we both started to laugh because the funny thing was, his name was actually Gabriel, so right after we both stopped laughing, I said to her, "It's so funny because that is what I named him." And with a smile, she replied to me and said, "That's a powerful name, he is Gabriel, the angel of God."

I then began to tell her about what the doctors told me about his diagnosis, and she said, "It is well my daughter,

God knows best." I also told her about the fact that his name was chosen eight years ago when I had my first son. See, eight years ago, after I had my son and I named him Dantae, something came into my spirit and said to me, "Your next son I will give you, I want you to name him Gabriel." At first, I never thought anything of it because I love that name, but it wasn't until I was faced with this pregnancy that I took the time to research the true meaning of the name Gabriel. Gabriel means God is my strength, and what amazes me the most was that if it weren't for the strength of God, I wouldn't have made it through my pregnancy alive. They were both blown away by this story, and believe it or not, when I first found out I was pregnant, before he was even diagnosed with his condition, it was already written on my heart that if he is a boy, his name will be Gabriel. So it became a reality because it was already designed by God before he was even formed in my womb; now, that is very powerful if you ask me.

My lovely friend's name is Antoinette. She became a very nice friend, too, on that day; she was the person who suggested that I should sign up with the midwives based on everything that I had told her about my OB visit. That same day, she told me everything I needed to know about midwives, and she even helped me to sign up with them that same day at her house. To be honest, I was extremely nervous at first signing up with midwives because I used my OB for my son, and then I connected with a doula for my daughter, and if I may say, the doula I got with my daughter was so amazing, because of the way she helped me, especially during my labour from start to finish, which was just incredible. Her name was Rhonda, and I will never forget her.

A few days later, I got an email from them, and I was told to call and book an appointment. In the email, they told me who I was assigned to, and immediately, I started to pray. I said, "Dear Lord, I pray they will accept me as a patient regardless of my baby's condition, and they will make sure they give us the best care possible." In my heart, all I wanted was someone compassionate towards my baby and me and someone who is sensitive about my feelings. Because I was going through as a high-risk pregnancy as a single mother, trying to do her best to raise her other two children on her own, I was facing the most terrifying pregnancy journey ever in my whole entire life. The next day, I decided to call and booked the appointment. The following week, I went in to meet my midwife. Her name was Katherina, and from the moment she approaches me, I knew I was in the right place because her passion for what she does shows on her face through her smile.

She took me to the room she was assigned to and introduce me to someone she was training, whose name was Emily. She was also very passionate about her career, which I could tell clearly just by the way she was smiling with me and the way she communicated with me throughout my appointment. We were there for around 45 minutes since they needed to do an intake to know more about my baby and me. At first, I was very scared to tell them about my baby's condition because, in my mind, I was so afraid they would treat me the same as my OB had. To be honest, that scared me very much, which is why I needed to tell them on my first visit.

During that first visit, they told me about what they do and don't do, and also what their aim is for each and every pregnant woman who chooses to be a part of their organization. She told me their aim is to provide the best care to both mother and child. Unlike other places, they are not there to make decisions for you, but instead, they will make decisions with you because, and she quoted, *"Only a mother knows what is best for her and her baby so therefore we are here to support you with any decision that is right for you."*

That day, I decided to go with them because I knew that they would provide my baby and me with the best care, based on everything that they told me. Also, I felt a very unique connection for some reason, with both of them in the room that day. Furthermore, at my next visit with them, they requested my permission to contact my previous OB to get personal information about my pregnancy and to be honest, I got so nervous I ended up leaving there without even signing the release form.

Later that night, Antoinette texted me asking me about my visit, and I told her what happened. She then told me, "Cemone, it's okay, they will not turn you away, in fact, they will be even more sensitive and compassionate towards you because they already know that you are going through a lot with a high-risk pregnancy. Trust me, Cemone, they will take great care of you, I promise you."

So, at my next visit, I opened up to them about my baby's condition and a little about my personal life as a single mother since they were asking me about the support system I had in place during such a difficult time. I was completely honest with them; I told them the only support system I had in place at that moment was a few Facebook mothers I connected with online after sharing my story through various groups looking for emotional support during my depression.. Also, I mentioned the few pregnant women I had met through the prenatal programs I go to when I am strong enough to go.

This pregnancy was by far the worst pregnancy of my three children. The pain, the suffering, the loneliness, the struggles,depression, the sacrifices plus on top of all that I was also feeling weak and sick all the time because I had little to no physical help, except when my new mommy friend, Dagmara, would come and get my kids every rwo weeks on a Saturday when she is off work .

She would drive to my house, pick them up and bring them to her house to play with her two beautiful daughters, both of them were so amazing with my two children. At times, I just felt like we were one big happy family because of the way they treated my kids and the way their mom looked out for me just melted my heart. She had no idea how much I truly appreciated her help. My own family and friends decided to ignore my pain and chose to make excuses as to why they couldn't help me with the kids during my darkest moments, yet Dagmara decided to be there for me as much as possible because she knew I was struggling and I had no other physical help.

Mount Saini hospital was recommended through a few Facebook mothers' groups after I made a post asking where I should go for the best care during a high-risk pregnancy. I was so shocked by how many people recommended that hospital on my post that day, so I decided to get my family doctor to send a referral for me there. The most amazing part of this was that my midwife also works with that hospital as well.

I was recommended to go the fetal medicine unit to join the special pregnancy program. I remember my first visit there. I had to sit and wait for over four hours to see a doctor because there were so many pregnant women there that day. My heart began to beat like crazy, it felt like it was about to jump out of my chest. The doctor I met with that day was Dr. Ryan and based on the amazing review I got about him online, I was very excited to finally meet him in person. I knew he worked for Mount Saini hospital even before I went there that day.

That day I had another ultrasound, and then I met with Dr. Ryan, who sat down with me and told me more about what to expect during my pregnancy carrying an Anencephaly baby. He explained that my baby would die either before or after birth, because unfortunately, he has no brain or skull developed and usually, babies with this condition cannot survive outside the womb. He then reminded me about my option to terminate, but unlike my other OB, he assured me that it was up to me. He also made it very clear that whatever decision I chose to make, they would be there to support my decision and make it their duty to provide us with the best care possible throughout the rest of my pregnancy.

At that point, I was in tears again because I was so heartbroken hearing all those things once again after hearing the same things months ago from my OB, but for some reason, I also felt at home because of the care he said I would be receiving for the rest of my pregnancy there with them as my secondary caregiver since my midwives were my primary caregivers.

At my next visit there, I met with a nurse who was assigned to help me create a birthing plan, a social worker who was assigned to tell me about different resources out there in regards to my pregnancy, and also a spiritual counsellor because they recognized the faith I had in God. They also knew that I trusted God's plans for my baby's life, regardless of his diagnosis with Anencephaly. I also met with another doctor who reminded me about my option to terminate again as well as the risk that could occur going through with the pregnancy. He also mentioned to me that in these cases, because of my baby's condition, they will make my health a priority, which meant they wouldn't put my health at risk to save the baby, knowing he would die anyway. That crushed my heart to pieces, to be honest.

Nothing hurt more than those words, so immediately, I just felt tears running down my face again. I didn't want to be put in a position where I had to choose my life over my own child's life, and just the thought of that happening broke my heart into pieces once again. He then reminded me that I was in good hands there, and they will make sure I receive the best care throughout the rest of my pregnancy with them. And again, that brought comfort to my heart and soul.

Each week I went there, I was treated with respect, compassion, and good care, since everyone there was extremely nice to me even though at times, they felt scared for me, seeing the size of my belly due to my baby's condition.

At that time, I was carrying around over eight extra pounds of fluid, which is why the doctor there recommended that I consider having a fluid reduction ASAP. The spiritual counsellor there helped me a lot emotionally, by talking with her each time I went there. It helped to build my faith, and it made me choose to trust the will of God even more for my baby's life.

I want to leave this with you. When I chose to trust God to lead the way, I didn't just receive good care in return, but I received the best care from start to end through everyone I was connected with along the way. Everyone who took care of me there and during my entire pregnancy was amazing because they were all sent by God.

My message to you is this: If you ever have to experience a pregnancy like mine or even similar to mine where people may treat you a certain way because of the condition of your baby, please don't accept it because both of you deserve the very best regardless of the condition of your pregnancy. I want you to make a decision that will ensure that you will only receive the best care possible for both you and your baby, and no matter what, never allow anyone to make you feel uncomfortable or guilty about making a decision that is right for you. Because, in the end, you will regret it if it wasn't what your heart desires for your baby.

Do not stop looking until you find the best care for you and your baby because only then will you enjoy the little time you have with your little one. My life wasn't perfect when I met these people, but it got much better, and that's a fact. I was no longer as depressed as I was before. I got through it only because I was surrounded by love and positive people.

It won't be an easy road, I will not lie to you, but it will feel much better than before once you are connected with the right support system. You will even find reasons to smile at times when you should be crying because that's how powerful God is. He will let you smile throughout your storms in life. And just so you all know, I never regretted seeking help. I only regretted waiting so long to seek it. But in the end, God knew best, and that is why I trusted His timing and not mine.

Chapter 4
The arrival of my mother in Canada

My mom's name is Gloria Neil. She is a single mother of eight children, including me. As a child, I remember watching my mother struggle every day, just to take care of us because, just like my children's fathers, our fathers also walked out of our lives and left her to raise all of us by herself. I cannot remember ever seeing my mother cry. In fact, I saw her smile and laugh more than ever seeing her sad. I will never forget the pain, the struggles, the sacrifices and the suffering she chose to endure just to put food on the table, a shelter over our head and clothes on our backs. She would get up every morning at 4:30 a.m. or 5:00 a.m. and get ready to go to work every single day because she knew that if she didn't do it, she would not be able to take care of us since she had no other help in place.

I am her youngest daughter; maybe that's why my life is so similar to hers. I never realized how hard it was to be a single mother until I went through it myself, and that made me love and cherish my mom even more. Looking at my life, I have noticed much the same pattern from my mothers' life. For example, we are both single mothers; we are both built strong, mentally, physically and spiritually, not to mention how we find ways to smile at each storm in our lives. Both my mother and I loved our children unconditionally, which is why regardless of how difficult and stressful it was and still is, raising our children alone, we were both determined to never give up on them no matter what.

My mother has always been the biggest inspiration in my life and not because she was perfect, because as we all know, no one is, but because she loved us. She was willing to fight for us no matter what; she might have made many mistakes with us but based on how we all turned out, she definitely did an excellent job raising all of us. She has always been a woman of faith and a woman of love, she loves to help others, and I find myself being her twin when it comes to that. I remember times when she would take her last bit of money and give it away to people, and I would get so angry because I couldn't understand why she would choose to do that knowing that she had all of us to take care of and no one else was there to help her.

She did it so much that one day, I decided to confront her about it. I said to her, "Mom, why do you always give away everything to others when you don't have much left, then; as a result, you have to work so hard to make it up, in order to take care of us?" She then replied by saying, "In this life, my dear daughter, for an act of kindness we do for others, God always rewards us in return." She said, "I may have just a little, but that person has none, so why would I allow him to go hungry when I know I am able to feed him?" To be honest, after that day, I started to see things differently, and it made me into who I am today.

Around three years ago, I literally had to force her to get her passport.. I hoped and prayed that one day she would decide to come here and spend some time out of Jamaica for once in her entire life. In 2019, a couple of months after her best friend, Miss Ivette, had passed away, something in my spirit led me to ask her again, and to my surprise, she accepted my offer. This was so shocking, but also very amazing, given the fact that she really needed a vacation, and I was happy to treat her to her first-ever vacation at age 66.

At that time, I wasn't aware that I was pregnant, but I knew she wasn't handling her best friend's death well, so I wanted to get her out of Jamaica for a bit in hopes that it would take her mind away from everything that had happened. Miss Ivette was like a second mother to me, and every time I went to visit my mom in Jamaica, I had to go and visit her at her house. She loved me like her own daughter, and she loved my two children like her own grandchildren. She always went out of her way every time I visited her to make me sweet potato pudding because she knew I loved it.

I was so surprised when I heard about her death, and I was so moved by the love she had for my family, which is why I had to spend all I had to travel there just to say goodbye to her. My heart was so broken knowing that she was gone, but most of all, I knew going back to Jamaica after her death wouldn't be the same, given the fact that I will never see her again, and that makes me very sad deep inside my heart.

My mom got very emotional after her best friend passed away, and both my older sister Melissa and I got very concerned about her, mainly because she was taking sleeping pills. Emotionally, she wasn't doing well since she was blaming herself for not making time to say goodbye to Miss Ivette. We knew that because she was no longer around, my mom didn't have anyone to talk to because Miss Ivette was her only real friend. They would spend countless hours at her house after she finished work each day, and they went everywhere together.

At the time when this happened, I was still working, so I decided to start saving just in case she decided she was ready for a vacation, or in case any emergency arose. A couple of months later, I decided to ask her if she wanted to come now, and to my surprise, she said yes. In shock, I asked her, "Are you sure?" I remember that for years, she didn't want to come because she was too afraid of flying on a plane.

My first thought when my mom accepted my invitation was that she wanted to get away from the pain of losing her best friend, but it wasn't until she got here in November of 2019 that I learned from her that it was the voice of God that led her to come. She told me that when I asked her this time around, something in her heart told her she should come because this was the right time, and that's why she decided to come.

She had no idea I was pregnant, nor did she know anything about my baby's condition; in fact, many people I knew had no idea. Only those I felt comfortable with knew. Many people begged me to tell her before she got here, but they didn't know my mom the way I did, so I chose not to. See, my mom likes to worry a lot, and she takes things to heart, which is why two years ago when I left my husband of ten years, I never told her anything about it.

I was here struggling and suffering all alone as a single mother with little to no help while still taking care of her financially, along with other family members in Jamaica, whenever they needed help. I remember around 15 years ago after I came to Canada and lived with my dad, my stepmom asked me to leave her house, even though I was only 17 years old. I had nowhere to go since they were the only family I knew here in Canada. I had to go to a shelter to live.

I was so scared that I called my mom, and I told her everything. Upon hearing that, my mom got stressed out since she took it to heart, and she fainted. They had to bring her to the hospital that day. I got so scared after I heard what had happened, that I made a promise to myself to never tell her any more bad news again over the phone. From that day, I have been carrying that guilt of almost loosing her, even now as I am writing this.

A few months later, I stopped working since my contract was over at my place at work. The next day, I had to go with my son for his surgery. I didn't have time to look into her visa until my son had recovered, since I had no help during that time. After my son recovered and was able to go to daycare along with my daughter, I decided to try to find another job. At the same time, I got someone to help me write a proper invitation letter to my mom, inviting her to Canada for a vacation.

My sister looked up the fee for the visa and everything else she had to pay to come to Canada. She sent me the total, and my head began to hurt so badly because the money I saved would all be gone just paying for the things my mom needed to come here, not even including her plane ticket. On top of that, it was around that time when I found out I was pregnant. Along with the horrible news about my son's condition, not only was I struggling to get my mom here, but I was also raising my children alone before I met those mamas online.

When my mom got approved for her visa, I was so happy and excited. I decided to share it in the group since they have been following my pregnancy journey all along. However, a part of me was feeling very sad because I knew I didn't have enough money to purchase her ticket right away. Since I used up all I had to get her visa and glasses since she was having eye problems and a few other things, I still had my two children to care for too.

During that time, I told a few people that I was trying to get my mom here, including my family and the church I went to, but no one offered to help me despite knowing that I wasn't working anymore. I was going through a difficult pregnancy, and I was raising my children all alone after my son's father walked away due to the baby's diagnosis of Anencephaly.

They also knew I was greatly in need of physical help because I had none at home besides my 7-year-old son. I must admit, my son Dantae is the best son I could ever have prayed for; not only was he taking care of his little sister when I needed to lay down, but he was also taking care of me too. He would get me a snack in bed, he would help me do laundry, he would help me clean up the house, but most of all, he was caring and compassionate to me.

He would pray for me when I could not pray for myself, he would pray for his little sister and brother as well as himself. He would always do this to make me smile whenever he noticed that I was a bit sad. I remember one day I was feeling so sick, and he came to me and said,

"Mommy, I wish I was older so I could do everything for you because you have done so much for my sister and me." He then continued by saying," Mommy, I know that you are sad because you always have to do everything, and you need rest." Then he said, "Mommy, I can't wait for grandma to come so that she can help you, and then you can rest." All I could do at that point was smile and gave him a hug and kiss on his cheeks and just remind him how much I love him.

Over the course of my pregnancy, I have always been very prayerful because it was only by the grace of God that I survived everything I encountered. I always try to put my trust and faith in God because I know on my own I wouldn't have made it. Believe it or not, the devil found many reasons along the way to end my life, but God always saved me from all his plots and traps.

I remember that many nights I would pray to God to make a way for my mom to come here so she could help me. I needed some physical help around the house and with the children desperately. Then something amazing happened. A couple of weeks later, I had a few moms reach out to me and offer to help me pay for her ticket since, from my story, they knew it was challenging for me to do it all alone. I thank God for the few mamas who helped me to purchase her ticket to come here because I wasn't able to afford everything on my own.

One week before my mom arrived, my niece dropped by and brought us some groceries. As we were there talking for the first time in ages, I told her how disappointed I was in my family for sitting back and watching me suffer alone, knowing everything I was going through. She told me that everyone has their own struggles, which I did agree with, but I said to her, "Even though everyone is going through their own struggles, offering help to someone you love and care about should be a priority, especially with a situation such as mine. None of you offered even to come and watch the kids for little bit, so I could get some rest."

I told her that, "I don't expect you to be here for me every day, but at least you could have tried to be here for me sometimes as my family who claim to love us so much." Don't get me wrong, this niece I am talking about has been my only real family here in Canada since I got here. She has done a lot for my two children and me since she is their Godmother, and I show her gratitude for her kindness in ways you would never imagine. Anyone who knows me well knows that I love to show appreciation to everyone who helps me, and it doesn't really matter if it's big or small, that's just who I am, and that won't change no matter what life brings my way. I have also helped her a lot too, because that's what you do when you love someone, at least, that's how I feel in my heart.

A few months later, after she accepted my offer, I managed to get her here with the help of a few wonderful mamas in the groups who offered to help me, after following my pregnancy journey in the mothers' groups.

Two days before my mom arrived, Grace texted me, and while we were talking, she asked me when my mom was coming, so I told her, and immediately she offered to come and pick me up with my two children and bring us to the airport to get my mother. I was so surprised by her act of kindness that I just started to cry. That whole week, I was praying and asking God how I could get my mom at the airport, being so tired and weak, but then, like always, God came through for me again.

Ever since my mom has arrived here, she has been taking care of her grandchildren and me and she has been a blessing for me throughout the last stages of my pregnancy. She was so shocked when she saw that I was pregnant, but then she was hurt hearing about his condition and what I had gone through by myself until God sent me all the help I needed along the way.

She watches me every day struggling as a single mother, and even though I was pregnant and in such pain, I was still making sure I got everything done for my children, along with making sure she was well taken care of in every way. This touched her heart so deeply that she actually broke down into tears. One day when I got home, she was crying, and at first, I thought something was wrong with her, but then I realized that she was only crying because she felt bad for me as she said, "All these years you have been taking care of your other siblings and me in Jamaica and no one knew how hard you have it here by yourself."

In tears, she said, "Cemone, you have it really hard here with no one helping you in the house with the children; you are a very strong woman." Then I replied to her by saying, "I got that from you because you have always taught us to be strong, so now I have to be strong ,if not for me, for my children because I am the only person they have."

My mom has been the strongest person I've known in all my life because I watched her for many years back in Jamaica struggling with all of us, so when I saw her break down in tears after a few months of watching me going through the same thing, she touched my heart so deeply in ways no words could ever have described.

I want to leave this with you and I hope it will inspire you the way it inspires me over the years.

You will never know how strong you are until being strong is all you've got.

Also, someone once asked me this, and it touched my heart; they said, "Cemone, you are so strong — how do you do it?" I replied and said, "I am strong because I chose to be, and it's not just for me, but also for my children who are relying on me." Find things within your life that will build your strength because, in this life, in order to survive, we have to find the strength we need to keep on going no matter what obstacles we are faced with along the way. Thank you, mom, for teaching me from a very young age how to be strong because even without you around, I am still able to stay strong no whatever what life brings my way.

Chapter 5
Life and Death Decision

Ever since my mom saw how huge my belly was getting as my due date got closer, she got worried about my health, mainly because of how hard it was to walk, sleep or even breathe properly. She would stay up at night with me since I could hardly lay down to sleep many nights due to the discomfort of the weight of my belly. Everyone thought I was having three or four children because of the size of my belly.

I remember on numerous occasions, both my midwife and my doctor from the hospital kept on suggesting that I should consider doing a fluid reduction so that my belly would get much lighter, I would be in less pain, able to move better, breathe better and also get a good night's rest but despite everything they were telling me, I could not find myself agreeing to do it because I was so afraid of hurting my baby in the process.

I remember my mom telling me a few times how worried she would get every time I left the house to go drop the kids off for school or daycare, get groceries, went to do Christmas shopping or even attend prenatal programs. She said, " I felt so scared for you being out there alone knowing you can hardly walk due to the size of your belly, it made it impossible for me to eat or sleep until you got home."

She continued by saying, "Since I had no phone to call you, all I could do is sit and pray to God that nothing happens to you out there." I wasn't able to afford a house phone or anything else at that time, because I had used up everything I had to get her here.

One day, after I got home with the kids, after a very long day outside in the freezing cold, my mom looked at me and said, "Cemone, you are a very strong woman, look at the weather out there, and look at your belly, and instead of staying home, you still found the strength to go out there and hustle to feed all of us." I remember she also said to me, "Even though I had it very hard in Jamaica raising all of you, at least the weather was good. But you have it much harder here. Even without help or support, you refuse to give up." I remember saying back to her in a very calm voice, "Mom, when I love someone, I will go above and beyond for them no matter the circumstances because, in my heart, I already know that everything I have sacrificed for you and my children will be worth it in the end." She then looked at me shaking her head, and said, "God will always bless you because your heart is so big and filled with so much love."

A few weeks later, my condition got so bad I wasn't able to walk for long because of all the pain I was feeling.

Since my belly was very heavy due to the amount of fluid in it, therefore I had to call Uber or a taxi to get around, and this now added more stress financially. My mom desperately wanted to help, but she was very new to Canada and outside was way too cold for her, so I knew if let her go out there in that weather, it would have caused more harm than good knowing that she is an older lady plus she already has knee issues which she has been struggling with for years living in Jamaica.

In the first week of January 2019 when I went for my regular check up at the hospital. Everyone there that saw me was very worried based on the size of my belly., I remember the person who did my ultra sound that day recommended that I do a fluid reduction immediately, because she was very concerned about the amount of fluid around the baby since it was very risky for my health.

Later on, when the doctor came in, he explained to me that if I chose to wait too long to get rid of some of the fluid, it could burst open my uterus and cause severe bleeding, which could lead to either death or having to have a blood transfusion. He told me it was best to do it that same day or ASAP because the longer I waited, the riskier it would become for me. This news broke my heart because I didn't want to risk my son coming too early or hurt him by doing that procedure. Based on everything they told me that day, one of the risks of doing it was that it might put his life in jeopardy since he could actually die from the procedure.

I was so confused and heartbroken that day, so I decided to reschedule the procedure for another day because I knew by agreeing to go through with the procedure could result in ending my son's life. I wasn't ready to say goodbye to my son yet, so I decided to go home. Later that evening, I was telling Maureen and the other mamas what had happened, and they all agree I should go in and have it done because I have to do what's best for my health.

The day of my procedure, Maureen took the day off from work to come and stay with me because she didn't want me to go through something so difficult all alone. My mom was home with my two children since I had no one to bring them to school or daycare that day, keeping in mind that I left the house at 6:00 a.m. because my appointment was at 7 a.m. Around 9:00 a.m. Maureen arrived, and she stayed with me throughout the whole procedure. Then she made sure I was recovered well before she left to go home. Unfortunately, I had to stay overnight to be monitored because, according to them, that was the best thing for me.

After everything was done, a nurse came to check my baby's heartbeat, and they couldn't find any. Immediately. I felt so guilty because I was told that this could happen, and I still went ahead because I wanted to save my life over his.

I started to pray to God, hoping that things would change, and to my surprise, a few minutes later, they found his heartbeat.

That night I could hardly sleep for many reasons, which included the fact that I missed my children very much. They had never spent a night without me before, and I knew my almost-three-year-old daughter would drive my mom crazy that night looking for me. I was also very afraid of his heart stopping again, so all I could do was pray and ask God to watch over him.

I remember, early the next morning, he was very busy moving around, and that made me very happy. That afternoon, when I got home and opened the door, my children seemed to know I was coming because immediately, they both ran towards me and hugged me. Then my daughter was just jumping up and down saying, "Mommy is home, Mommy is home." and then my son looked at my belly and said, "Mommy, where is Gabriel?" and I said, "He is still in mommy's tummy," and the smile that came over his face was priceless.

I had tried talking to my son a few times about his brother's condition, but every time I mentioned it, he would start crying. That just broke my heart to pieces seeing how emotional he was getting over the possibility of losing his brother, so I decided to stop. He was very excited when I told him he was having a little brother, and he developed such love for him during those few months. This is why it was hard for him to hear that he may die, so instead of talking about it, we would pray every night for his brother, and he enjoyed doing that a lot. This made me very happy. I also told him that if God should take Gabriel from us, he would be our personal angel here on earth, who would always be watching over us, and he looked at me and said. "Mommy, that sounds pretty amazing!"

Midway through my pregnancy, I also had a Toronto Public Health Nurse who was assigned to me through one of the prenatal programs because they knew I didn't have much support at home. She only visited my home once in a while, but I must admit she was a very lovely lady both inside and out; her heart was so pure, and her soul was so compassionate towards me especially after she found out everything I was going through with my baby. Her name was Allie.

She would come and check in with me to see how I was doing, and that meant a lot to me. After a few months of getting to know more about me, she then recommended a home care worker to come and visit me too every two weeks; whose name was Juliet. Both of them have been such a blessing in my life because they were so caring and compassionate towards me.

After his fluid reduction, they recommended that I come to the hospital every week as I was 35 weeks. I went there each week, and his heart was still beating, so at that point, I felt everything was going to turn out just fine. My midwives contacted me on the 16th of January, asking if it was okay to come to do a regular checkup the day after; I wasn't feeling well, so I told them to come on Saturday instead.

I remember that morning when I got up, I was still not well, so I was thinking about cancelling the appointment, however, they insisted on coming to see me, so I finally gave in. While they were there doing my checkup, they realized my son Gabriel had no heartbeat, and that is when it hit me.

My heart felt like it stopped beating because I knew if I hadn't had that fluid reduction, maybe he would still be alive, but then in my heart, I also realized that perhaps if I hadn't had it, then it could have been me who had died that day instead. Even though it hurts me deeply losing him, I knew it would have hurt my children more, losing me. They only have me, and that alone brought peace to me, knowing that I made the right decision not just for me alone, but for his big brother and his big sister.

I would like to leave this with you. At times in our lives, we will be faced with some very difficult, heartbreaking decisions that may result in leaving us feeling guilty. But, I am here to tell you never to feel guilty or carry the burden of not forgiving yourself for making a decision that is right for you despite the outcome of that situation. In the end, everything happens for a reason, even though, at times, we may not see it right away.

Chapter 6
The Death of My Son Gabriel

They kept trying and trying, but there was no heartbeat. With my heart so broken into pieces, trying to process this news, my midwives suggested going into the hospital to confirm it with an ultrasound. I was so confused because that same Wednesday, I went to the hospital to do an ultrasound, and he was alive, but now on Saturday, he was gone. On our way to the hospital sitting in her car, I was just hoping and praying that this was just a misunderstanding, and my son was still alive. I remember posting in the mothers' group and asking my mama friends to pray for a miracle, but unfortunately, that was indeed the end of his life.

Based on the ultrasound, he had no heartbeat and right then and there, they told me if I wanted, they could induce labour in order to deliver him. I told them I needed a moment to take this in, so they all left the room, and all I could do was cry, with a million things going through my mind.

I was still not ready to say goodbye to him because, in my heart, I was really hoping that God would change my story and allow him to live far beyond what all the doctors were saying. But, to be honest with you, the thing that hurt the most that afternoon, was knowing that after all the pain, the struggle and the sacrifices I had made, he was taken away from me before I even saw his face. The thought of not hearing him cry, seeing him move, watching him open his eyes and having life in him crushed my heart into pieces.

My heart couldn't understand why God chose to take him away from me before I even got to saw his face. From the moment I heard about his condition and the outcome of what could happen, my only desire was that either God made him a healthy baby, or He let me see him alive, for even an hour or less.

That evening I decided to go home because I was way too heartbroken to even think about seeing my son born lifeless. Not only that, but I knew my body was way too weak to even undergo induced labour. In my heart, I felt a bit of relief knowing that he died peacefully inside, but my heart was in so much pain knowing that when he comes out, he won't be alive. Those thoughts made my head hurt so badly, and the hardest part for me was I had no one there at that moment to even turn to for emotional support. I knew my midwives were outside, but for the first time going through this pregnancy, I actually wished I had a spouse there for me to turn to after losing my baby. Unfortunately, since he had walked away, I had to face that tragic moment alone.

Moments later, my midwives came back in. They were both so caring and compassionate; they hugged me and told me they were sorry again for my loss. With tears running down my face and my heart feeling as if it was going to stop, I couldn't even respond to them at that moment. Instead, I just sat there and cried for a bit more. After I finished crying and gained back a little strength, I decided to text Maureen and tell her what had happened. She was so concerned about me that she wanted to come to the hospital that same evening, but because I had decided not to go through labour and delivery that evening, I told her she didn't have to come because I would be going home in a few minutes.

On my way home that evening, I told a few other people that have been by my side throughout my pregnancy about his death, and everyone was in shock. We were all hoping for a miraculous turn around despite everything that was so obvious to us. I knew deep down that this could have happened based on all the things I underwent, for example, the building up of the fluid around him in my womb and the sickness I struggled with throughout my entire pregnancy, but because I wanted a miracle so badly, I ignored all the signs to actual reality.

When I got home, my heart was so heavy walking through the door because I wasn't prepared to tell my children that their brother was gone, my daughter was too young to understand, but I knew it would affect my son deeply because he had developed so much love for his brother throughout the course of my pregnancy. My mom knew what had happened as soon as I got home without me even telling her anything; she saw in my eyes that I was crying though I was trying to smile for my children as they greeted me at the door.

I wasn't ready to accept that my son was gone; neither was I ready to face the reality that he won't be physically here for the rest of my life. I remember walking into my room, closing the door behind me, switching off the lights and crying myself to sleep because I wanted the pain I was feeling to just go away.

I remember waking up a few hours later, and when I saw my other two children, I felt so blessed, but at the same time, I felt sad because I knew the one I had in my womb had been taken away from me before he was even born. Something in me appreciated my other two children even more at that moment because I don't know how I would have survived losing my son if I didn't have other children to love and cherish in my life going forward.

I got my children ready for bed that night, and after they fell asleep, I sat up all night with my mom talking and watching movies. She was so worried about my physical health that she basically begged me to go in the following day to have the baby. I remember that morning, I texted

Maureen as the day before, she told me that whenever I was ready to go have the baby, I should let her know. She said she would be there with me no matter what, and she kept her word.

I also texted my midwives and a few other people about my decision to go in and have my baby. My midwives called the hospital and made all the arrangements for me so that when I got there my room would be already available for me.

My mom literally begged me that morning to get some rest because she was so concerned that I wouldn't make it through labour and delivery if I were too weak. She made me breakfast that morning, and she told me to go to sleep, so I listened to her and went to bed. I got up around 2:00 p.m. and told her, "I will get ready now and go into the hospital." I texted Maureen and told her I was ready to go in, and without even thinking, she replied, "I will be there in an hour's time."

That evening, while waiting on Maureen, I remember being so heartbroken knowing that this was not a dream, but instead, it was reality, my son Gabriel was really gone. I sat on my bed and prayed to God for the strength to go through this because I felt emotionally destroyed and physically drained, and to be honest; I just wanted everything to be over and done with. Unfortunately, I was up for way more than I could have ever imagined.

Maureen texted me a few minutes later saying she was outside, and immediately this sadness came over me because I knew not only did I have to spend the night without my children at home, but also, I was going to meet my other son lifeless, and that almost made me cry. I then hugged my mom and my children, and when I opened the door, there she was standing there with a big smile on her face. To be honest, even though it was a very difficult time for me, just seeing her smile lifted up my spirit and immediately, I felt my self-smiling too.

I got in the car and greeted her husband, and for the whole journey to the hospital, we were all talking and laughing, and for a second or two, I wasn't thinking about my baby being gone; instead, we were actually talking about life in Jamaica, one of my happiest places to be in this world besides Canada. Upon arrival at the hospital, I thanked her husband for dropping us off, and we went to meet my midwives, who were already there waiting for us.

I will leave this with you. Never feel guilty about things over which you have no control; instead, feel proud within yourself-knowing that you have done everything you could on your part, and that should be enough to carry you on no matter what the outcome may be in the end. Also, remember that everything in our lives has a reason for happening, whether it's good or bad, so never stress over what you cannot control.

Chapter 7
Delivering My Stillborn Son

We got into the room, and they gave me my hospital clothes to change into. While I was changing, I started to remember the birth of my other two children. Immediately, that sadness came back over me again because deep down, I knew, unlike my other two deliveries where they were born alive and crying, this one will not be anything like that. Just the thought of knowing what the outcome would be brought tears to my eyes once again.

I got dressed, then went to lie down on the bed. Then a nurse walked in and greeted me and offered her condolences and told me not to worry because everyone there will make sure I get the best care during my entire visit, and she was absolutely right. From start to finish, everyone who cared for me treated me like royalty, so even though it was a very sad occasion being there, they made sure it was an incredible experience, one which I will never ever forget.

The nurse explained to me what they would be doing throughout the night, and then a doctor came in to make sure I understood everything clearly before they started my inducement. My midwives and my friend Maureen were there, making sure I was comfortable and receiving the best care possible, and at that very moment, despite everything that had happened and also that which was about to happen, in my heart, I knew I was blessed beyond words. My heart felt at peace, knowing that I was surrounded by so much love and support.

Before they started to induce labour that night, I got some visitors. The first set was my older sister and my older niece, who had just finished church, so they decided to drop by and wish me a safe delivery before they went home.

My niece was the only reliable family I ever had here in Canada, which is why I was so hurt and disappointed when she allowed me to go through that painful and heartbreaking pregnancy journey as a single mother all alone without trying to help at all. Both of us faced many challenges together, and because of that, we became very close over the years. She has been there for her Godchildren and me whenever she could, and in return, I was always there for her as well because that is what family should do for each other, especially in times of need. I have grown to admire her very much because of who she is; my niece is a very loving and humble person who has a very huge heart for helping others despite what she is going through in her own life. That made her a very special person in my life because we had so much in common.

My next visitor that night was one of my new mommy friends whose name was Dagmara. Ever since God brought us together, she has been a blessing in my life and my children's lives. She has impacted my life in more ways than one, compared to many people I have known for many years, especially with my children and that alone touched my heart deeply. This act of kindness from her during the short time I have known her has opened my eyes to realize that in this life, it's not how long you have known people; instead, it's the impact they have chosen to make in your life that really counts in the end.

She stopped by for about five minutes that night because she was actually working close by the hospital, and according to her, she just wanted to come and give me a hug before I went through one of the scariest moments of my life. I had many people checking in on me during this time on my phone, especially my other new mommy friend Grace. She has been so amazing to me from the moment God brought her into our lives, not only that, but I remember looking at my phone, and everyone in the mothers' group were all praying for me. In that moment, I knew regardless of how difficult this process was going to be for me, God was with me, and I was not alone.

My nurse came back into the room and gave me pills, which I took orally, to start my induction process, and it took forever even to kick in. But, because I had Maureen there to talk to, it didn't really matter to me as much since we were there talking and laughing about this show that was on the TV called *90 Day Fiancé*. As time went by, the medication was taking so long to work that after my 6th dose, they decided to switch from oral to vaginal and by the way, just so we are clear, this was actually after a full 24 hours. The main reason why they had to do a very slow induction for me was because of the amount of fluid that was in my womb, due to my son's condition. They didn't want it to tear open my uterus if the pressure was too much because that could have caused severe bleeding for me, which would have lead to either death or needing a blood transfusion in the end,

After they switched the medication to vaginal, the labour process began to improve, and that's when the pain started. After a while, it just got so unbearable that I wanted something to stop the pain immediately. I knew this pregnancy really took a lot out of me because with my other two children, I had the strength to go through 22 hours of induced labour with my son and six hours of natural labour with my daughter without asking for any medication at all, but with Gabriel, I knew my body was not able to handle it.

Gabriel's pregnancy journey had me weak emotionally and physically, so I knew I had to take the easy road this time by requesting an epidural. Unfortunately, that was indeed a huge mistake in the end. It took them two tries to even get the epidural to go into my back because, according to the doctor who was doing it, my spine was not normal, so they had to use an ultrasound on their second time to locate where to put the needle in to avoid any complication.

They finally got the epidural in and taped up my back, and immediately, my water broke. The pain I was in was so intense, that all I wanted was the epidural to start working, but unfortunately, within 15 minutes, before the epidural could even kick in, my son Gabriel was ready to be born. I remember being in so much pain that I almost passed out before he was born. After he came out, I heard a big splash of water that came out after him that soaked the bed and flooded the floor. Immediately, it hit me to the core, once again, because deep down, I knew my son was gone forever.

I lay there just waiting to hear him cry, and to hear the doctor's shout he is alive. I wanted that miracle I had been praying for throughout my whole entire pregnancy so badly, but in the end, I didn't get a miracle. Instead God gave me an angel, who has been watching over us ever since. I was very disappointed in God for taking my son away, but I was also thankful that I had 38 weeks with him to love and cherish him in my womb.

Giving birth to Grace was by far my best and easiest of all three children simply because I had a fantastic doula with me all the way to the end, whose name was Rholanda. I always talk about how amazing she was, because, to be honest, her skills in that delivery room were just incredible from beginning to end, and I thank God everyday for blessing my life with her that day.

All I wanted was at least one day with my beautiful son Gabriel, especially because of all the pain and suffering I endured, and all the sacrifices I had to make just to give him a chance at life. My only desire, in the end, was to hold him while he was alive, but unfortunately, I was denied that opportunity, and that really broke my heart.

About an hour later, I asked to see my son, nervously waiting while they brought him in, covering his head with the green hat I brought in for him. He was wrapped in a green and white blanket I had bought specifically for him because my favourite colour is green. I wanted him to be connected to me someway or somehow. I held him in my arms, and surely as I looked at his face, he looked just like his brother and his sister, which immediately melted my heart. My greatest fear was the way he would look after all the pictures I saw online with his diagnosis, along with the fact that he had passed away in me over four days ago. I was terrified, but I thank God that in the end, he was a handsome baby boy who I loved unconditionally.

I sat there smiling at my son, and in my heart, I felt so peaceful knowing that despite everything I went through carrying him, I never gave up on him. I gave him life in my womb for 38 weeks because I knew deep down, based on his diagnosis, he wouldn't have gotten a chance to live after he was born. I made a decision as his mother, who loved him unconditionally despite his diagnosis, to love him and carry him as long as God allowed me to do so because, in my heart, he was worthy of my love and so much more.

One of my midwives decided to capture many precious moments of me holding him so that I would have them to cherish with my family after I left the hospital and going forward without him being here physically.

They also did a photoshoot for us as part of a memory package at the hospital, which included footprints, photos of him, a necklace in my favourite colour which spelled his name, and a few more heartwarming gifts for me to bring home with me, once I leave the hospital.

Baby Gabriel was born on January 21st, 2020, at 2:16 a.m., weighing 4 pounds and 13 ounces. Everything else in my womb was only fluid, which is why when I delivered him, there was a massive flood in the room that morning due to the large amount of fluid around him in my womb.

Later that day, I had three visitors. The first one was my Toronto Public Health Nurse, Allie, who came by to offer her condolences. She brought me a book to start my writing journey because she knew that my desire was to write a book about my pregnancy journey to honour my son Gabriel and also to use as a tool to help others in the future.

I told her that my son Gabriel had inspired me to finally follow my dream of becoming one of the best authors across the world because I know that all my stories will be powerful enough to change lives and make a difference in this world.

She was so sweet and compassionate towards me once she got there that for a quick moment, I actually forgot what had just happened because I was just there smiling and having such a nice conversation with her. A few minutes later, Grace came, and I introduced them to each other. Immediately Allie knew who she was because I always talked about her and how amazing she has been to my children and me ever since we got connected through that Facebook mothers' group.

She brought me a beautiful yellow flower, and for a moment, I wasn't heartbroken or sad; instead, I felt so happy and blessed to be surrounded by complete strangers who have chosen to love and supported me during the darkest moments of my entire life. They spent a few hours with me there, and after they left, I got my final visitor for the night. Her name was Debbie; she was also from a mothers' group called Black Mom Connection, and Grace and Dagmara were from another one called Mumming.

Debbie walked in with a big smile on her face holding a green bag in my favourite colour, and that had me speechless because I had never told her what my favourite colour was. But somehow she had chosen to bring me gifts in it, and that's when I knew God was still at work in my life despite everything that had happened with my son.

Our conversation flowed so naturally, it felt like I knew her for years even though that was, in fact, our first meeting there in the hospital. Before she left, she prayed for me, and she also gave me a green energy drink to drink that she picked up on her way there to see me.

After she walked out of my room that evening immediately, a sadness came back over me again because I started to remember everything that had happened with my son earlier that day. The thought of him passing away broke my heart. I tried my best to fight the tears from coming, but because of all the hurt I was feeling in my heart, I just had to let it out.

Later that night, I asked to see my son one last time because I knew that in the morning, it would have been too hard for me to see him before I left the hospital to go home. I lay there with him in my arms, and I watched his beautiful face as he rested there in heavenly peace and even though I didn't get to meet him alive, I knew in my heart he felt my love for him for 38weeks in my womb and that alone made my heart happy in the end.

The next day, Grace came to take me home and while I was walking out of the hospital, my heart literally stopped beating for a second or two because I felt so much hurt and pain knowing that my son will be left there all alone. I never knew my heart could hurt that much until I left him there that day. I wanted to take him home with me, but I couldn't because I had my other two children at home, and I knew it would only make things worse if I should bring home a dead baby.

That same day, I asked Grace to take me to the dentist's office to book an appointment for my two children because I had missed their last appointment because I was too big to even walk during my pregnancy. I remember when the lady at the front desk saw me, she said to me, "Congratulations on your pregnancy." Then I smiled at her and replied, "I just gave birth yesterday." She was so shocked to see me even walking around that she replied, "Why are you here? You should be in bed resting." I smiled with her and said, "I'm going home now."

I also asked Grace to take me to the grocery store too, because I knew my kids and my mom needed food in the house. I went to get food for them myself. I remember being in so much pain, which was making it difficult to walk but regardless of how I felt, I knew that wasn't going to stop me from feeding my family.

On the way home, I also got pizza and fries for the kids because that's something they both love to eat. I knew my mom would have cooked anything that's there for us to eat, so I wasn't worried about us at all. Anyway, as we got closer to my house, I felt so sad because I knew my son would be expecting to see his little brother Gabriel, but he was gone. I wasn't prepared how to approach it; neither was I ready to see him mourning the loss of his brother that he had grown to love so much over the course of my pregnancy.

I got home and opened the door, and as soon as I entered, my daughter ran to greet me; the joy she felt seeing me and the happiness she had on her face made me realize how blessed I was. My son also came and hugged me, and just seeing the sadness in his eyes, I knew my mom already shared the bad news with him.

Grace helped me bring all the groceries inside, then she gave me a hug, and she left. I could not even look at my mom, or stay with them, so I went straight to my room, closed my door, turned off the light and cried myself to sleep.

Later that evening, I got up, and my mom begged me to eat something, so I did. Then my son came to me and said, "Mommy, I know that Gabriel is dead because grandma told me." Immediately, I saw tears running down his face, so I just held him in my arms, and we just cried together for a little while. My daughter saw us crying, and she began to cry too; even though she didn't know why we were crying, she just didn't like seeing us hurting, and at that moment, I knew my life would never be the same ever again.

That whole night I couldn't sleep, so my mom and I stayed up to watch movies and talk about life because I needed something to get my mind off everything that had just happened.

I want to leave this message with you, and I hope it will touch your heart as you read it. Never be afraid to cry whenever you feel the need to do so, especially after you have lost someone so close to your heart. There is no shame in crying over someone you love because that is the best way to heal from all the hurt and the pain which your heart is feeling while grieving someone you love so dearly.

Moreover, try to always surround yourself with people who will uplift you and show you love and compassion during those difficult moments of your life because it will make a big difference for you in the end. Also, make sure that you always make decisions that are right for you and never allow the pressure of someone else's opinion to make you feel guilty about what you really need in your life because, in the end, only you will have to live with your final decisions.

Lastly, whenever you listen to your heart and do what is right for you in the end, you will feel peace and have a clear understanding, but whenever you allow others to make decisions for you, in the end, you will only feel guilt and confusion, which is not what you want or need.

Chapter 8
Funeral Arrangements

This was one of the hardest things I have ever had to do in my entire life because I still could not believe that my son Gabriel was really gone. I kept on telling myself that this was only a dream, and one day I would wake up, and my son will be alive and well, but unfortunately, that never happened.

Many nights I couldn't close my eyes to sleep because of all the hurt and pain that I was experiencing after the passing of my son. At times, I felt like I abandoned my son, knowing that I left him in the hospital all alone. These feelings haunted me everyday, and even though I knew he wasn't alive, it still bothered me a lot because I knew he wasn't laid to rest. I felt like I should've been there with him until I was able to bury him.

I felt as if I was in a horrible nightmare, and even though I wanted to wake up, I couldn't, no matter how hard I tried.

Have you ever been so hurt by something in your life, that even though you wanted to cry, there were no tears to cry? Well, that was how I felt at that moment.

I tried my very best not to think about him being there in that hospital all alone, but as his mother, I could not help it because I wanted to be there with him until I was able to lay him to rest.

I remember my mom, my son and a few other people trying to cheer me up, but nothing was able to fill the emptiness that was in my heart. I was in so much anguish that, at one point, I felt as if I couldn't even breathe properly.

My very first visitors after I got home from the hospital were my two favourite people from my previous job.

They came to my house with flowers, food and a big hug, which were very much needed because I was going through a very dark time. I needed to be reminded that I wasn't really alone. Katie was the best boss I ever had; not only was she loving and caring, but she was also very down to earth and hilarious. This is why we had such a great friendship before I stopped working there. Sarah was the best co-worker I ever have had, not only because she was funny, but also because she was just a very nice person inside and out.

They were a blessing in my life during the time I worked at Oasis Community Center.

I will never forget what was written on the card with the flowers they delivered to me because the words really touched my heart to the core, not only because I loved working there, but because almost eight months after I left, they still remembered me and still considered me to be a part of their family.

In the card, they wrote, "Cemone, our hearts go out to you during this very difficult time, and we want you to know that you are in our hearts and prayers. From your Oasis family."

That visit not only put a smile on my face, but it also made my heart smile because I knew that they cared about me even though I was no longer working for them.

I had a few more visitors afterwards, and that actually made me realize how much people were touched by the passing of my son Gabriel.

A few mothers from the prenatal program, New Mamas, that I met on Facebook in mothers' groups visited along with my midwives, my Toronto Public Health Nurse Allie, my in-home care worker Juliet, my pastor, and some family members.

Despite all the pain I was going through emotionally and physically, I still had to find the strength to help my mom celebrate her first birthday here in Canada.

Even though she didn't want me to stress myself out anymore, I just couldn't allow her birthday to pass without making sure that she enjoyed it.

Many people during this journey have told me, "You have been an inspiration to me, and not only that, but you are the strongest woman I have ever met in my entire life."

The things I have encountered in my life have made me into the woman I am today, which is why I try my best every day to be strong, not only for myself but for the ones I love dearly.

I do not have many friends, but I thank God for the few God has brought into my life. They have been a great help to both my family and me.

Graciela, who I met during my pregnancy, is a great friend, not only because she has been there for me, but because she is a beautiful person inside and out.

For my mother's birthday, she was the one who came and picked us up from our house, drove us to the restaurant, picked up my mom, and drove us back home. Keep in mind that she was very sick that day, but she didn't allow that to stop her from helping me to make sure my mom had a great birthday. Now that is what you call a true friend indeed.

I had my stillborn son on January 21st. On the 22nd, I was doing grocery shopping, and on the 26th, I was out with my mother celebrating her 67th birthday.

No one will ever understand how hard this was for me, but I knew my mom deserved the best birthday life could offer, so I made sure she received it.

The smile on her face while we were singing happy birthday to her melted my heart so deeply because, after everything she had done for me, I know the sacrifice I made for her that day was so worth it.

My mother, Gloria Neil, is a selfless person just like myself, which is why I know without a doubt that she is my mommy.

After we got home that evening, my mom looked at me and said, "God is going to bless you in so many ways because you have a good heart." Hearing those words from my mother touched me to the core.

That night. I wasn't able to sleep because I knew it was time to start finalizing my son Gabriel's funeral. I wasn't ready to be planning a funeral, but ready or not, I had to get it done.

I felt so overwhelmed calling different places to compare prices and trying to get a good resting place for my son.

I had no family by my side, helping to plan my son Gabriel's funeral except for my mom, who was new in Canada, and my two small children.

I remember while I was getting things together, my eight-year-old-son Dantae came in and asked, "Mommy, can I help you with my brother's funeral?" I was so surprised when I heard him ask that, but I was also happy too because I wanted him to be a part of his little brother's funeral.

We started to design a collage with pictures of Gabriel and made notes that we pretended to read to him as if he were there, and to be honest, for the very first time since he had died, I felt peace in my heart. I was doing something meaningful and special for him, along with his big brother.

We even did a poem that he read at the funeral along with my goodbye note to my handsome son Gabriel.

We ended up making many things to put in his little casket and also to display at the funeral service. This was very good because it helped me to heal, and it also helped me to connect with my son Dantae on a deeper level concerning his feelings towards the death of his brother.

I must admit, he was much stronger than I ever expected him to be, and even now, after everything is over, he is still handling his brother's death very maturely.

After we completed everything for the funeral, I helped him to practise his poem for his brother's funeral.

Not many people can imagine how hard it has been for me to not only lose my son but to have to find the strength to help my other son.

My daughter, who was almost three at the time, still doesn't understand exactly what has happened yet, but I know without a doubt, very soon, I will have to explain to her everything that happened to her little brother.

I know deep down my life will never ever be the same again, but I thank God for his love for us.

That night, just like many others, I did not sleep well because I couldn't stop thinking about the death of my son. I tried my best to take my mind off it, but I just couldn't, and it made me so sad. Many times I found myself questioning God because I wanted to understand why my son had to die, and why I wasn't even given a day to spend with him after everything I had to endure during my pregnancy.

I had many questions but no answers, and this just broke my heart even more day after day, until God spoke to my heart one night while I was in my room on my bed with my face staring at the ceiling and tears running down my face.

I heard this voice say to me, "The reason why I took him before he was born was that I knew it would have hurt you more watching him dying in your arms. I love you too much to let you go through that knowing it would have shattered your heart into pieces."

At that moment, for the first time in a long time, I felt the peace of God, and I knew I would be okay. That night I prayed and thanked God for never leaving me alone because I knew, without a doubt, that He was with me from the beginning. And just like that, I slept like a baby.

The next day my midwives came to check up on me, and they were everything and beyond what I could have ever imagined them to be. They were loving, caring, compassionate, and understanding, but above all, they were excellent at their job.

Their names are Catherine, Emily, and Elizabeth. They work for the Midwives Collectives of Toronto. Anyone living in Toronto, Canada that needs a good midwife, I highly recommend them. Based on my experience with them, I know you will be in good hands.

Miss Ronalda was an angel sent by God into my life; she was there when I really needed her to be there for me. I remember after I spent days and hours calling and finalizing my son's funeral arrangements, basically by myself at home, I was so worried that I might have to go to the funeral home alone. It scared me so much because I was still trying to accept the fact that this was really happening to me. I remember for the first time, I said it out loud, My son is gone, and I am planning his funeral. I never thought in a million years that this would have been my life, but guess what? It was, and it is, so I made a decision to give him the best funeral I could because I knew he deserved it and more.

Many people were telling me to cremate him, but that wasn't what my heart was saying. To be honest, I am so happy I followed my heart and not what others were saying to me because now I am at peace with all the decisions I have made from the time I found out I was pregnant to the day I laid him to rest.

It is very important for us to do things in this life which will bring us peace and not regrets. Many people around me were pressuring me to get an abortion, but I knew what I could and could not live with, so I made a decision to follow my heart. In the end, God took care of me by sending the right people at the right time to help me through my difficult pregnancy journey with my son Gabriel.

At times, I wish I had made time to build more memories with my son before God took him home, but nevertheless, I know in my heart, he felt loved by me, his big brother and his big sister. While he was growing in me, I made sure they got to talk to him, feel his kicks and kiss my tummy. We used even to sing to him, pray for him and anoint him inside my womb; this was our little family bonding every night before bed.

My son dreamt about his little brother twice, and he cherishes those dreams even today because he truly loves both his siblings very much. I remember the first time he dreamt about his little brother Gabriel; he was so happy telling me about his dream. He said, "Mommy, I dreamed that Grace and I were playing with Gabriel in the living room, and he was so cute." At that moment, I started to smile, knowing that he will always remember his brother in that way and not in a scary way due to his diagnosis with Anencephaly.

I did everything I could in this life to make sure I never gave up on Gabriel because I loved him regardless of his diagnosis, and in my eyes, he was my son, and I loved him unconditionally with everything thing in me and more.

Planning my son's funeral made me realize how truly strong I was, not just physically but also mentally, emotionally, and also spiritually as well.

I remembered I wasn't working, my son just died, and I was raising two children with hardly any money. A few people offered to help me raise money; some people were nice, but others were so heartless.

BMC {Black Mom Connection} Mothers' group was one of the biggest blessings in my life because the mothers in that group helped me to fight depression, fed me after I got out of the hospital and helped me to get around since I was unable to walk due to the size of my belly while pregnant. Moreover, that group blessed me with a few mama friends who are still my friends today and thank God for that!

I was a member of a few mothers' groups, but just a few of them live up to the expectation of what a mothers' group should be. Black Mom Connection was the best out of all of them, mainly because they never judged me, never criticized me, were always checking up on me, and they treated my kids and me like family.

The night before I went into the funeral home, I was so sad because I knew I had to go in to finalize the paperwork for my son's funeral. But I didn't want to go alone. Since I am not the type of person that usually reaches out for help, I had made up my mind to go there alone because my mom would have to stay home with the kids since it was winter, and my daughter was only two years old.

I remember that night, while I was there trying to prepare myself mentally and emotionally to go to the funeral home the next day, I got a message from Ronalda. She wanted to check in on me, and without holding back, I told her everything I was feeling, and I will never forget how amazing she made me feel afterwards before I went to bed.

The next day, she came and picked me up, brought me to the funeral home, sat there with me to be the voice I didn't have during those moments of nervousness and shock. I was literally speechless while I was there looking at the box they would put him in, listening to the details of the service on the day of his funeral.

I remember she asked me, "Would you like to carry your son from the service to the car that will bring him to his final resting place?" My heart stopped for a few seconds.

Then I answered, "Yes, I would love to carry my son in my arms for the last time before I lay him to rest." My heart was beating so fast thinking about it because I was so scared of dropping him or not being strong enough to actually hold him in that box, but in my heart, I knew this was something I needed to do, not just for him, but also for me and his brother and sister. Ronalda was there by my side through the whole thing, even though she needed to go to work. She was willing to sacrifice money, just to be there with me, and that is when I realized I was not alone because someone always cares, even if they are not my blood family.

Sitting there in that funeral home, planning my son's funeral made me realize how short life really is, and it broke my heart. My son wasn't even given the chance to be born alive; he never got to see my face or the faces of his brother or sister before he died. At first, I was scared to go in there, but after a while, I said to myself, "I am the only one who can give my son the funeral he deserves," so I started to tell them what I needed for my son. And I left there knowing that my son would be given a beautiful service because I always go above and beyond for all my children.

After we were finished there, Miss Ronalda took me for a cup of coffee. I will never forget the person who served us put a heart in my coffee, and that made me smile because I was just so surprised that he knew that I really needed to see that at that moment; so I looked up, and I said, "God I know this is you."

While she was driving me home that morning, I looked across at her, and I couldn't believe that she was late for work, just to be there with me while people who were closer to me all made excuses. So I thanked her for going with me, then she told me, "Whatever you need, always remember that I am here for you, and with you as long as you need me, I will be here to help you."

She dropped me off. I thanked her once again, then I went into my house and there they were at the door, my two babies waiting to hug and kiss me. They heard my keys opening the door, and they rushed to the door because they knew it was me, and they were super excited to see their mommy.

That night I was at peace knowing that my son's funeral was almost ready, but I was also a bit sad knowing that he was really gone, and there was nothing I could do to bring him back to life. This thought took my breath away just for a moment because I knew I would never get to see his face ever again except on the pictures I have of him or if I dreamt about him, and this broke my heart to the core.

The next day, I went shopping for funeral clothes for me, my son, my daughter and my mother, which was so hard because I felt so heartbroken. I wanted to cry so badly, but I had to fight it because I didn't want anyone to see me crying and then start asking me questions. Mentally and emotionally, I wasn't ready to talk about the death of my son; I just wanted to get through the day without breaking down into tears in the middle of the mall.

That day, I found a beautiful dress for my little daughter, Grace, and I bought a nice suit for my son, Dantae, and that alone made me very happy. That night, I spoke to a few people as they were all checking in on how I was coping after the death of my son Gabriel. Many people loved him, even though they never got to meet him before he died because he has touched many lives all over the world through my incredible journey with him.

I decided to name him Gabriel Angel Rowe because before he was even created, God gave me his name Gabriel eight years ago after my son was born. Angel is because he has died and became our earthly angel paving the way for me and his big brother and sister, and Rowe my last name, because he had no earthly father.

Later that evening, the funeral home reminded me that I had no pastor to do his funeral because my pastor wasn't available the day I chose to do his funeral. They suggested that they could find me a pastor to do it, but I didn't want that. I wanted the right pastor, who could do a beautiful service for him because I knew he deserved the very best. I also needed a photographer to capture some memorable moments of my last time with my three children together, and immediately, Nicole came to mind.

Nicole is someone I knew a while back. She had done a few photoshoots for me before, so I knew she was the perfect person for the job. That evening, I reached out to her, and I told her what was going on, and she agreed to do it for me. If anyone out there is looking for a great photographer, who is not only talented but is also very passionate and beautiful inside and out, I recommend you check her out if you want really good work done for memorable moments.

That night before I went to bed, I prayed and asked God to connect me with the right pastor who would give my son Gabriel the best funeral service. Sure enough, God heard my prayers because the next day, I was talking to Allie, my Toronto Public Health Nurse, about my situation as she called to check in on me. From our conversation, she referred me to a pastor she knew, and I must admit, he was definitely sent to me by God.

His name was Pastor Riley; he was everything I had prayed and hoped for from God. Our conversation on the phone was so natural; I felt as if I had known him for many years, even on the first day we connected. I told him a bit about my story, and he said to me we will pray, and God will take control of everything.

That same day, I spoke to a few people who were coming to the funeral. Most of them were people I met last year while I was pregnant with Gabriel. Even though it was a very sad occasion for my family and me, I was so thankful to God because he never left my side, and he brought the right people into my life at the right time.

The next day I got a call from the Stop Community Center; this was one of the prenatal programs I used to visit while I was pregnant with Gabriel. I will never forget that conversation because my heart was touched so deeply, knowing how much they cared about me and the death of my son.

After my son died, I wanted to go back to the programs or even call and tell them what had happened, but I just couldn't find the strength and courage to face anyone or say the words out loud because deep down, I was hurting so much.

I was struggling so much emotionally because a part of me wanted my son to be alive and well. I didn't even want to leave my house; I felt much better being inside where I didn't have to face anyone who would ask me questions about my son that I wasn't ready to answer.

I remember, even for school and daycare, my mom had to sacrifice her health to go out in the winter to drop them off and pick them up for me because I didn't want to go there. It was my mom's first winter in Canada, so it was very difficult for her, and that is when I had to face my biggest fear of facing people again for the very first time.

The first time I brought them to daycare after the death of Gabriel was the hardest because by then, everyone knew what had happened. Everyone wanted to give their condolences, and that made me so uncomfortable because now it felt real more than ever before.

Eventually, my guard was breaking down, and I didn't feel uncomfortable anymore. Instead, I started to feel proud because I then realized that there was nothing wrong with talking about someone I loved unconditionally.

The Stop Community Center invited me in to talk, so I went in. At first, I got a bit emotional and overwhelmed because I saw so many healthy babies there, but my Gabriel was gone. For a minute, I wanted to just walk out and never go back, but I fought that feeling, and I stayed.

I met with this lovely lady, whose name is Christine. She was the one who had called me on the phone because she knew me very well, since I also visited there with my daughter, Grace, over two years prior to that.

I ended up talking to a few of them, and they offered to buy the flowers for my son's funeral and to be honest, I almost broke down into tears.

I left there not feeling scared or afraid anymore not only because they comforted me but because I was able to talk to a group of people who knew Gabriel and me on a very personal level; they watched me from when I was weeks pregnant, all the way to 38 weeks when he took his last breath.

That evening I went home, and for the first time, I was more open to talking about his passing, and it got me emotional, but not in a bad way, but instead in a very good way because now I was ready to talk about my journey with him. This was very inspirational and motivational to many people, and that has even inspired me to write this book, which I know will touch many lives across the world.

The funeral arrangements were completed, the date was set, and Grace volunteered to drive us to the funeral service.

As I looked at my mom's face that night and the faces of my children, I knew right then and there that our lives would never be the same again. Even though it felt a bit scary, in my heart, I wasn't afraid because I knew I wasn't alone, and therefore everything was going to be just fine.

That night my mom and I stayed up while the kids were sleeping, and we watched television and laughed and for a few hours, I wasn't thinking about my son's funeral; I was just spending quality time with my mother. Our favourite TV show to watch was NCIS Los Angeles with LL Cool J. She loved the little old lady in it so much. We spent many hours watching it because that took my mind off everything that was going on in my life.

This experience brought us closer than ever before, and I cherished every moment of it. My mom Gloria is a lovely person inside and out, and her faith in God is what I admire the most about her. I remember at times when I would be feeling a bit discouraged; she would always say this to me, "God knows best, and he will never give you more than you can handle in this life." Even today, when she is in Jamaica, and I am here in Canada, at times, I can still hear her voice in my head whenever I feel a bit discouraged, especially on specific days like the day Gabriel died, the day I gave birth to him, and the day I laid him to rest.

CEMONE ROWE

We watched television until around 3:00 a.m. in the morning; then she insisted that I go and get some rest because the next day was going to be a day I would never ever forget, the day I would lay my son to rest and say goodbye to him until I see him again in the next life.

Chapter 9
Gabriel's Funeral Service

Gabriel was loved beyond words, and not even his death could stop me from loving him unconditionally. His brother and sister didn't have the opportunity to meet him alive, but they shared very special moments with him while I was pregnant and those memories we will cherish forever.

I remember that morning; I got up feeling very emotional. I wanted to cry, but I couldn't find the tears because my heart was hurting so much. I didn't know how I was going to get through that day, but I knew I wasn't going to let anything or anyone ruin this very special day for my beautiful baby boy.

My mom and my other two children were my rock that day because despite everything I was experiencing emotionally, looking at them brought so much joy to my heart. My mom was so helpful that morning, and my son Dantae, he just always puts a smile on my face on days when I feet like crying. He is indeed the best son I could ever have asked for in this life. Not only is he loving and caring, but he is also very helpful to both his little sister and me. He is the kind of son that gets up every day and puts a smile on my face regardless of what I am going through. He would tell me how beautiful I look and how amazing I am to him and his little sister Grace. I remember one day walking them to school and daycare before work, and out of the blue, he said, "Mommy, you are the best, you do everything for my sister and me and when I get older, I will take care of you."

That morning as I got my daughter dressed along with myself, I took a deep breath, and I said to myself, "I can do this because I know I am not going to face this day alone." I had God, my mother, my children and a few wonderful people by my side.

My wonderful new Mommy Friend, Graciela, volunteered to take us that morning to the funeral service even though she lived almost an hour away from us. She has been a blessing to my family and me in ways words cannot explain, which is why I call her my chosen family.

Getting dressed that morning was extremely difficult, not just because it was my son's funeral but because I didn't know how my other son would handle seeing his little brother for the first time in a little box. I had already explained to him what to expect, but I was still concerned about him because I knew how much he loved his brother.

He was so excited when I told him I was pregnant and that it was a boy, and it broke my heart, knowing that his brother is no longer here with us.

Watching him getting dressed that morning broke my heart to pieces because after almost nine months of waiting to meet his little brother, he will now meet him at his funeral.

As we arrived at the funeral service that morning, I was so surprised to see how many people were already there. For a second, I felt so guilty because I knew deep down that I should have been the first to arrive, but nevertheless, I was happy seeing so many people there waiting for me.

I saw a few people from my Oasis family, Katie, the best boss I ever had in my life, Richard, my other boss who loved drinking very hot tea, Sarah, the best co-worker I ever had in my life, and last but not least Nicholas. This man was someone very special to my heart, not only because he treated me like his little sister, but because I've watched him fight through so much. I felt so blessed, knowing that God had used me to impact his life the way I did, and because of the bond we created, he showed up at my son's funeral.

The next person I saw there was Maureen, the mother who stood by me through some of my darkest moments during my pregnancy; she is also one of my chosen family. Also there were Nicole my photographer, Rolonda, who helped me finalize my son's funeral arrangements, and Allie, my Toronto Public Health Nurse, whose smile just melts my heart every time I see her.

I will admit that at first when I arrived, I was very nervous and a bit emotional, but after seeing all these people there and seeing more people arrive, immediately, I knew I would be okay.

I met pastor Riley for the first time that morning, and I knew he was sent to me by God. We were finalizing how the service would go, and to be honest, all my fears, all my worries, all my emotions just disappeared. The only thing that was on my mind was giving my son the best funeral because that is what he deserved. I also met pastor Riley's beautiful wife with an angelic voice, who blessed my son's funeral with a few songs. She sang so well that people were actually crying because it got so emotional as the service went on.

As I walked into the room where my son was that morning, my heart almost jumped out of my chest, seeing him in that tiny box, and then it hit me, Gabriel is really gone forever. They gave my children and me five minutes alone with Gabriel before the service began, and that's something I will cherish for the rest of my life.

My mom was not emotionally ready for everything, so she sat in the back with Miss Allie. I sat at the front alone with my two children. Moments later, my daughter Grace ran off. At first, I thought she was going to my mom, but to my surprise, she went to sit with Dagmara and her two daughters, because she really loves them very much. My daughter never came back up to the front until I was reading my goodbye note to her little brother. She ran up to me, and I picked her up as I read what I wrote to him. I remember I started to cry as I was reading, and my daughter was there, wiping my tears away. As I looked up, almost everyone was in tears, including my eight-year-old son Dantae, and that broke my heart.

After I went to sit down beside my son , my daughter ran off again to sit with Dagmara and her beautiful daughters, so that gave me the chance I needed to comfort my son. I wiped his tears away and I told him that I loved him. My son went up to read his poem to his little brother. As I sat there watching him, I knew my life would never ever be the same again.

He read the poem so beautifully that people even started to cry. I wanted to cry too, but I fought it because I had to stay strong for my children. During my speech, I couldn't hold back my tears because it cut me so deeply, remembering the sacrifices and hardships I endured for almost nine months only to watch my son go down in a grave.

As the service went on, I found myself staring at his little box, and all I could think about was the time I held him in my arms in the hospital. I kissed his little cheeks, held his fingers and told him about his brother and sister. I know this might seem a bit weird, but I had to do everything my heart told me that night because I knew if I didn't, I would live in regret after I buried him.

As Rolanda read a scripture, she broke down into tears, and it touched my heart so deeply because my son had impacted many people even though he was gone. Pastor Riley did an incredible job with my son's funeral service from start to finish, to the point where people thought he was my pastor.

After the service was finished, I said goodbye to a few people because they were not able to come with us to Gabriel's grave.

I noticed my niece was there, and the associate pastor of my church. They both gave me a hug and an envelope as they left to go to work. I also realized that a few people I had met while attending prenatal programs where there, too, including Dagmara, who purchased the flowers for my son's funeral.

My heart was touched so deeply when I saw one of the mothers I met at the prenatal program, who came with her little baby, just to pay her final respects to my son Gabriel, whose name is Daniella. She is a very beautiful person inside and out, which is why even today, we are still friends.

Many people told me how strong I was, but the truth is that God was my strength; I was praying in my spirit throughout the service just telling God to take control because the human side of me wanted to break down everytime I looked at my son in that little coffin, just lying there lifeless.

Many times, I wanted to just rush up there, and take him into my arms and kiss his forehead and hold his little finger, but I knew if I did, that I would ruin his beautiful funeral service. I had to fight my emotions and smile through all the pain my heart was feeling.

I had many wonderful people there, so even though it was a very sad occasion, I was smiling my way through everything my heart was feeling about losing my son.

People thought I was strong, but to be honest, the strongest person there was my son Dantae. At the age of only eight, I was so impressed with how he conducted himself throughout the whole day.

At one point, I saw a line of people waiting to hug us, and immediately, I knew I was not alone; I was surrounded by people that loved Gabriel so much without even meeting him. Now that is powerful.

I have never received so many hugs in my life, but I loved every single one of them. After most people were gone, something in my heart told me to get some markers, and you would not believe what happened next.

Both my children began to decorate their little brother's box with hearts and notes. Then we wrote our names on it. I was so impressed at the end because it was just so beautiful and colourful.

My daughter was almost three, so this was the perfect way for her to get involved with her brother's funeral. My son Dantae, looked so happy and peaceful decorating his brother's box, to the point where it melted my heart just watching them saying goodbye to their little brother.

Everyone that was there was so amazed how creative they were together. I always taught them the importance of working together to achieve things in life, even before my daughter was able to talk.

People have always admired the bond they share. It's something that I teach them almost every day. Family, to me, is very important because, for most of my life, I felt as if I had none.

After Dantae and Grace finished decorating their brother's box that afternoon, it was time for me to carry him to the car. At first, I was a bit nervous because I knew it would take so much strength to hold his box, knowing that these were our last moments together on earth.

I took his box in my arms, and walked out of the service holding him closely. My daughter Grace was in front of me, Dantae beside me on the left, and my mother on the right. Behind us was Dagmara, her daughters, her mother, Gracelia, Rolanada, and a few other people.

I approached the car and put my son in; then I thanked my photographer for coming because she had to go to work. She is such a talented photographer; I was so impressed with all her photos and videos because she captured some really great moments for me that day. Even today, I cherish them all, with all of my heart.

My mom and my daughter Grace drove with Graciela. My son, Dantae, and I drove in the limo, behind the one with Gabriel, to the cemetery. On our way there, I had some time to talk to Dantae, and I must admit, he is very mature for his age. He said, "Mommy, my little brother is now in heaven with God, and he will be watching over us every day because now God has given us our own angel here on earth."

It was a very cold, snowy day, but that didn't bother me because my mind and heart were only on my son's funeral and being there for my other children if they needed me. As we arrived at the cemetery, I knew it was time to say goodbye to my beautiful baby boy; and that thought pierced me so deeply, as no one in this world could heal that hurt.

I got out of the limo and walked towards his car and took him in my arms one more time and started to walk towards his grave, even though it was freezing cold and my fingers were burning. All I could focus on, at that moment, was my son in my arms because I didn't want to slip and fall with him.

My mom stayed in Graciela's car with my daughter, Grace, because she fell asleep, and it was way too cold to try to bring her to the grave in that kind of weather. My son, on the other hand, was by my side the entire time, while I was walking with his brother's box in my arms for the last time. He was walking right beside me with the roses Ronalda got us to go in the grave with Gabriel.

As I approached his grave with his box in my arms, I almost passed out when I saw where he was about to go. Until this day, I do not know how I stood strong when all I wanted to do was break down and cry because the pain of seeing that little grave crushed my heart.

As they took him out of my hands, my eyes were filled with tears. Even though I felt so weak, I knew I had to remain strong, not just for me, but for my sons. As I watched them put him down to be lowered into his little grave, I turned to look at my son, and the sadness on his face broke my heart to the core, so I pulled him close to me and wrapped my arms around him and gave him a kiss on his forehead. Then together, we placed the roses from Ronalda on his little brother's box and watched them lower him down into his grave.

For a moment, it felt like I was in a dream or watching a movie because never in my life would I have imagined that this would be my life. The love I have for my children cannot be expressed through words, but sharing this will give you an idea of just how much they mean to me.

After they finished lowering him down in the grave, I took a shovel and began to throw dirt down into his grave and again, my eyes were filled with tears, but I know no one noticed because it was freezing cold that day. I had no gloves on, but I made sure my son Dantae was warm from head to toe. I remember that Ronalda came over and gave me her gloves because I guess she noticed my fingers freezing.

I felt no cold that day because all my pain was in my heart, watching my son in that grave after everything I had endured and sacrificed, just to give him a chance at life.

I stayed there until they covered his grave, then Dantae and I put some beautiful flowers on his grave. The flowers were from Dagmara and her daughters and the Healthy Beginnings prenatal program inside the Stop Community Center.

As I stood there looking at the flowers on his grave with my arms wrapped around my other son, I felt the voice of God whisper in my heart and say, "It is finished."

I walked away from his grave that afternoon with peace in my heart, knowing that despite everything I encountered while carrying him, I never gave up on him or my other children, and that is why, even today as a single mother, I am still going stronger than ever before because his journey has made me stronger and much wiser than ever before.

After we left the cemetery, Graciela brought us to a beautiful restaurant to get my mind off things. To be honest, my heart was so happy because I was surrounded by so much love. At the restaurant, there were Dagmara, her daughters and her mom, along with Ronalda and my family, including my lovely mother, Gloria.

We sat there for hours just talking and laughing about different things. We ate great food and even though it was a sad occasion, I felt so blessed that I was able to share that special moment with some great people, especially my mother. Before my mom came to Canada, I had never been in a restaurant with her, so this was very special for both of us.

My mom dislikes funerals, so I knew this experience was very difficult for her, because after all, Gabriel was her grandson who she never got the chance to meet.

I do not have many people in my life who I can call friends, but these ladies proved to me that day, after my son's funeral, that they were not just my friends, but they were my chosen family from God.

They not only kept me company that evening, but they allowed me to shift my focus off the death of my son, and truly enjoy that evening as a big family. My mom was so happy that day, and despite everything I was going through, seeing a smile on her face made my heart smile.

We took so many pictures that day, which I can go back and look at now. Trust me; these pictures are so special to me because not only does it help me to remember my son, but one day I know my little daughter Grace will want to see her brother, and these pictures will be the only thing I will have to show her.

My son didn't get the opportunity to see his little brother before his funeral because I was afraid of scaring him. I know he is very emotional, so I wasn't sure how he would react, knowing that his brother couldn't move, open his eyes, cry or breathe. I know my son well, so I had to make a decision that I knew both of us could live with in the end.

I made sure I took pictures of Gabriel at the hospital so that whenever Dantae was ready to see him, I would have something to show him. I knew sooner or later, that conversation would come up, and he would become curious about what his brother actually looked like. Believe it or not, that was indeed what did happen.

After we left that beautiful restaurant, Ronalda offered to drop us off at home , so we all hugged and went our separate ways. Then just like that, everything hit me again as I walked through my door. I knew right then and there that my life would never be the same again because not only was I a single mother, but I was also a grieving mother as well. That night, I could not sleep because I was getting flashbacks of everything that had happened. For the first time since he died, I really wept. My pillow was soaked with tears; my head was hurting like crazy; my heart felt like it was going to drop out of my chest. The worst part was having no one to comfort me, or to cry with me over our son, because his father walked away 11 weeks ago. Up to this day, he never looked back even to see if we were okay or not.

After Gabriel's funeral, I was a complete mess for a few days. I couldn't eat or sleep well because I truly missed my son so much. I wished I could have him back in my life because I didn't know how to live without him. I was so emotional and I needed someone to talk to who could relate to what I was going through but no one was able to so. I decided to seek grief counselling, hoping that would help me to get through my grieving process. I did for a bit, so if you are reading this and you have lost a child, please seek counselling. It helps a lot to be around people that can relate to your pain and emotions after losing your bundle of joy.

However, if counselling is not for you, then find someone you could confide in because talking about your feelings and emotions will definitely help you to heal from the pain and heartache of losing the baby you loved so much.

After my son died, I thought my life would be over, but to my surprise, it was just the beginning of something incredible. I was invited one week later to the most amazing event of my life, the Magnetic Entrepreneur World Record attempt, by a lovely lady named Rosemarie Sanchez, who is a beautiful woman inside and out. That event changed my life because not only was I invited there, but my bio was included in the *Magnetic Entrepreneur World Renowned* book used in the Guinness World Record successful attempt, and that was the beginning of my journey of becoming an author. I was able to meet the magnificent Robert J. Moore, and a few other wonderful authors who inspired me even more to pursue my dream of becoming a best-selling author.

At first, I didn't see it, especially when my mom left to go back to Jamaica, and I was left to raise my two children all alone again while still grieving my son's death. I almost fell back into depression again, but God sent me another angel to shine light into my life right when I needed it the most. Her name was Marcia Everbless Campbell; she reached out to me after seeing everything that I been through and invited me to an event she was going to attend. I was so touched by her words to me that day, and I decided to go with her and believe it or not, she took care of me like her little sister.

I remember I got Daniella to watch the kids that day for me, and when I arrived at Marcia's hotel, the first thing she asked me was if I was hungry. She bought me lunch, then she took me for a wonderful night out, and for the first time in a very long time, I was enjoying myself. I spend all my time taking care of my children, so it felt good doing something for me that day. I won't lie, I missed them a lot, but I knew they were in good hands.

Anyway, that day, she invited me to The International Women's Achievement Award Ceremony because she was one of the recipients receiving an award. Marcia is a beautiful woman, and I felt so blessed that day because not only did I have the best time of my life, riding in a limo, meeting famous people, but I also got the opportunity to meet Miss Donna Gowe, one of biggest names in Jamaica today, along with some stars from the *Days of Our Lives* soap opera.

Before my mom left, The Lord spoke to my heart to donate everything I got for my son to help the poor. So the money people blessed me with from my son's funeral, I used to pack two barrels to send to Jamaica, plus I started to help seniors here in Canada with groceries and home-cooked meals through My Good Deeds Charity Program called Blessing Others as God Blesses me.

Now, every time great things happen in my life, I always look up to the sky and say, "Thank you, God, and thank you Gabriel," because I know without a doubt that His purpose in my life was to pave the way for me and help me become what God has created me to be in this world.

I have been through the worst, so I will not allow anything or anyone to hold me back anymore. I will trust and let Him guide my steps as I walk into my destiny with the help of my guardian angel, Gabriel.

We all miss you, Gabriel, but as your older brother would say to me every day, "My brother is our angel on earth, and he will always be with us where ever we go because even though he is gone, we are still a family forever."

You are not alone

I may not be able to take away your pain

But I am here to tell you that someone does care

When you feel like your whole world is falling apart

Always remember that God is holding you in his arms

When you want to talk but no one is near

Just remember that God is just a prayer away

Don't be afraid to cry when you are hurting

Because that is a sign to God that you need him there

Hold on to your faith even on your hardest days

CEMONE ROWE

Because in the midst of the storm God will put a smile on your face

So do not worry and never be afraid

Because in the midst of your darkness God will be your light

My message to someone reading this book is never to be afraid to face your fears in this life even if it makes you feel uncomfortable at times because through that transitional process, you will not only heal from it, but you will also help someone else in the world to heal from your story.

It will be difficult at first, but that's okay; you do not have to rush it, just take your time and do it the way you know is best for you, not what others feel is best for you.

Talking about what you are feeling will help you to accept what has happened, and it will draw the right people to you as you share your pain and struggles. Not only that, but you can also motivate or inspire someone out there in the world who didn't have a voice to be heard through your story as you decide to share it with the world.

Always remember that everything that happens to us in this life has already happened to someone, is happening to someone or will eventually happen to someone. So as we share our story, we will now help someone who needs it.

I was inspired more than ever to not only become the author I have always wanted to be, but I was also inspired and motivated to be someone who could touch lives through my stories and be everything that God has created me to be and more.

This journey has taught me many things, and I made a decision about what I choose to take and what I choose to let go. I learned to cherish every moment because life is very short; I learned never to allow my fear to cripple me, and finally, I learned that even in bad circumstances, good can come from them. This journey was horrible from start to end, but it made me stronger, it connected me with some lovely people, it inspired me to pursue my dream of being an author, and it allows me to build a stronger connection with God.

Only you can decide what you want from every situation in your life; I suggest that you choose the good and not the bad because from that you will be unstoppable.

To Gabriel, our angel in heaven

Dear Gabriel: This is your family, your mother, Cemone, your big brother, Dantae, and your big sister Grace. Words can never describe how much we miss you, and that is why life here on earth has been very difficult without you. We know that God is taking good care of you for us, but not being able to see you breaks our hearts so much. We never got the chance to see your eyes; neither did we get to see your beautiful smile, but one thing we are thankful for was the opportunity to see your handsome face, and that alone was enough for us to carry in our hearts and cherish these memories every single day.

I miss you so much, my little brother, and I wish every day that you were here to play with Grace and me. Grace doesn't know much about you, but I promise one day, I will tell her everything she needs to know about you, and I know she will love you as much as I do too. Seeing your pictures after you died made me cry because I never got the chance to say goodbye.

So many things I wanted to say to you I didn't get the chance and so many plans I had for us that are now gone. I dreamed about you more than once before you died, and that was the hope that kept my mommy alive. In my dreams, you were perfect and happy, and whenever I told our mommy these dreams, she would always get so happy. The smile on her face just melted my heart, and the hope in her voice made me realize how much she truly loves us all.

We cherished every moment we felt you kicking because that let us know that you were alive and were listening. I remember anointing mommy's tummy every night, and then we would all take turns to pray for you because we cared for you as a family. I cried so much when you passed away, because I wasn't ready for you to leave us just yet. I was very sad at first, but after I spoke to our mommy, then I understood why God took you so soon. She told me that even though we loved as much we did, God took you because he loved you even more. See, we prayed for a miracle, but he gave us something even better because now we have our own personal angel watching over us. I love you so much, my little brother and your sister loves you too, but above all, our mommy loves you even more.

I carried you not because it was easy but because you were worthy of unconditional love. I never regretted my journey with you; I only regretted not spending more time with you. I wish I had more time to tell you I love you and time to build more memories with you, but now that you are gone, I can only cherish the memories we had. I never knew what it truly meant to be selfless until you came into my life, which is why I was willing to die, just to give you a chance at life.

If my heart could connect to yours right now, I would like you to know that your family loves you more than words can ever express in this life. You may no longer be with us physically, but you will always live in our hearts forever, and even though you are gone from this earth, you will never be forgotten because your memories will forever live on.

So until we meet again, my son, just know that your mother, your brother, and your sister love you now and

CEMONE ROWE

forevermore because you will hold a very special place in our hearts until the end of time.

Love mom, brother and sister.

Made in the USA
Columbia, SC
20 October 2020